Twenty-Five Ways to Increase Sales and Profits Without Spending an Extra Dime on Advertising

Twenty-Five Ways to Increase Sales and Profits Without Spending an Extra Dime on Advertising

Richard Johnson

Crisp Publications, Inc.
Menlo Park, California

Twenty-Five Ways to Increase Sales and Profits Without Spending an Extra Dime on Advertising

Richard Johnson

CREDITS
Project Editor: **Kelly Scanlon**
Editor: **Jane Doyle Guthrie**
Page Layout: **Rod Hankins and Premila Malik Borchardt**
Cover Design: **Fifth Street Design**

©1999 by Crisp Publications, Inc.
Printed in the United States of America by Bawden Printing Company.

www.crisp-pub.com

Distribution to the U.S. Trade:

National Book Network, Inc.
4720 Boston Way
Lanham, MD 20706
1-800-462-6420

This book is printed on recyclable paper with soy ink.

99 00 01 02   10 9 8 7 6 5 4 3 2 1

Library of Congress Catalog Card Number: 97-67312
Johnson, Richard
Twenty-Five Ways to Increase Sales and Profits
Without Spending an Extra Dime on Advertising
ISBN: 1-56052-548-7

Contents

Value-Added Section

Introduction

Within your company exist "hidden marketing assets." These are often overlooked and many times not leveraged or optimized in ways that could make your company earn more money and operate more profitably. Such assets include your current marketing, salespeople, staff, customer base, relationships, and day-to-day policies and procedures.

The twenty-five ways to increase your sales and profits described here are designed to keep you from spending more money on advertising. They simply tap into the "hidden marketing assets" your company already has and help you use them more effectively. Some of these strategies will be easier to implement more quickly than others. Do these first and then work on the others. Your company probably already has someone on staff who could work with these strategies without a significant investment of time, energy, or financial resources. In fact, different employees can be assigned to work these strategies, increasing their profitability.

These strategies are not presented in any particular recommended order except for the first one. The USP or *unique selling proposition* should be established first to best optimize the effectiveness of all the other strategies. Each strategy discussed is organized in the following format: an overview of the strategy is presented, followed by specific guidelines for implementing it, and then a checklist is offered to help you implement the approach completely and in an effective sequence.

Your Marketing Evaluation

The first thing to do before implementing any strategies is perform a simple marketing evaluation of your business.

Often, as a business owner, manager, or employee, it's easy to get so involved in day-to-day operations that you overlook many of the marketing assets just sitting there in your business.

Uncover Your Hidden Marketing Assets

"Hidden marketing assets" may take many different forms, and if you can leverage and optimize them, they can produce $10,000 to $1,000,000 or more in additional revenue and profit for your business.

Using the following checklist, identify the marketing potential you think your business has:

_____ Past customers

_____ Present customers

_____ Special knowledge or expertise in your industry

_____ Unique product or service

_____ Underperforming salespeople, but inside and outside sales

_____ Advertising that doesn't presently get results

_____ Good relationships with vendors and suppliers

_____ A high percentage of satisfied customers

_____ Knowledge of the conversion rate of prospects to customers

_____ Knowledge of the average unit sale amount or average invoice billing

_____ Products or services that can be offered after the initial sale

_____ Good community relationships

_____ Prospective customers

_____ Good location

_____ High level of employee or staff expertise

_____ Knowledge of the competition's strengths and weaknesses

_____ Unique packaging or combination of products and services

_____ Good relationships with complementary businesses

_____ A great story to tell about your business or products

_____ A clearly defined target market or demographic group

_____ Successful advertising or marketing in the past

_____ A product or service on the "leading edge" of your industry

_____ Unique efficiencies in the operation of the business or production of your product

The more of these possibilities you checked, the more leverage you can receive by better optimizing your assets. By implementing the twenty-five strategies offered in this book, you will optimize all of your business's marketing assets and increase your revenue and profit. All without asking you to invest a great deal of money or to make a lot of costly and time-consuming changes in your operations.

Grow in Three Ways!

The genius behind these strategies and their success is that as they optimize and leverage your marketing assets more fully, your business grows in three ways all the time:

- Increase in prospects

- Increase in the conversion rate of prospects to customers

- Increase in the value or worth of each customer

Can your business experience more growth? Perhaps even exponential growth? The following exercise will tell you.

Define your present situation.

Present gross sales $_____

Desired growth   _____%

Desired gross sales $_____

Know your key ratios. It is important to determine as closely as possible your current average customer worth and closing or conversion rate. These ratios help you define your present situation and determine your growth potential.

Average customer worth or value over one year: $_____. Many times this information can be captured and tracked by computer. If you don't have this capacity, make a rough calculation as a starting point. (Take the number of times a customer buys from you during a year and multiply that by the amount of the customer's average purchase.)

Closing or conversion rate: _____% (within your current marketing and sales effort, at what rate you convert prospects—those who come into or inquire by phone about your business—into customers or clients)

Number of customers last 12 months: _____ (gross sales/ average customer worth)

Number of prospects last 12 months: _____ (number of customers/closing rate)

Complete a growth matrix.

	No. of Prospects Annually	Closing Ratio	No. of Buyers	Average Customer Worth	Gross Sales
Present Situation					
1. Increase Prospects					
2. Increase Closing Ratio					
3. Increase Customer Worth					
Do All Three					

Total net growth you will realize: $_____

Net Growth $_____ /

Present Gross Sales $_____ * 100 =

Actual Exponential Growth Achieved _____%

Here's an example:

	No. of Prospects Annually	Closing Ratio	No. of Buyers	Average Customer Worth	Gross Sales
Present Situation	1,500	30%	450	$2,222.22	$999,999
1. Increase Prospects	1,800	30%	540	$2,222.22	$999,999
2. Increase Closing Ratio	1,500	36%	540	$2,222.22	$999,999
3. Increase Customer Worth	1,500	30%	450	$2,666.66	$999,997
Do All Three	1,800	36%	648	$2,666.66	$1,727,996

Total net growth you will realize: $727,996

Net Growth $727,996 /

Present Gross Sales $1,000,000 * 100 =

Actual Exponential Growth Achieved 73%

If you can improve just a little in each of the three areas, then you can see very dramatic growth overall. Here is the exponential growth you will achieve at various levels of improvement in each area:

Growth in Each Area	Exponential Growth Achieved
10%	33%
15%	53%
20%	73%
25%	95%
30%	120%

Determining Your Unique Selling Proposition (USP)

Overview

If the owners and employees cannot explain why a company is in business, it's a cinch the customers and prospects won't know. If they don't know, they soon forget why they should do business with the company and over time will stop.

The *unique selling proposition* (USP) is simply a definition of why your company is different from any other in the industry. Is it service? Quality? Price? Exactly why did the owner go into business, and why do customers patronize your company? The USP sets your company apart and makes it unique in the marketplace. Call some former and current customers and ask why they do (or have done) business with you. If they tell you it's service, then get more specific and ask them what it is they like about the service. If they say quality, then ask them what it is they like about the quality.

In other words, be specific. The founders of Domino's Pizza knew they had to distinguish theirs from every other pizza store. How did they do it? They didn't say they would have faster service—they said Domino's will deliver pizza in thirty minutes or less *or it's free*. That's Domino's USP. In its television and newspaper ads Northwestern Mutual Life Insurance clearly indicates that its dividend performance is superior to that of any other insurance company. Not just that their investments pay off well, but more specifically that their dividends are higher. That's a unique selling proposition.

What is your company's USP? Is it a guarantee? Is it attractive financing? A certain furniture store manufactured and sold its own furniture. This was its USP, what separated that furniture store from any other. All marketing and advertising made it clear that this furniture store offered its own furniture and therefore a superior quality and guarantee.

Find out what makes your company unique from others by talking to employees, customers, and management. Find out why people do business with you and describe it in ninety words or less. You may of course have different USPs for different product lines—you can't be all things to all people. And you don't always have to be number one. Rather then battle Hertz for the top spot, Avis created a USP by calling itself the best number two car rental agency in the world and stating, "We try harder at Avis."

If your company is a hardware or grocery store that stocks the same hammers and saws or food as all your competitors, you can distinguish your business through your employees. Perhaps your employees are better trained or have more experience in the field. Perhaps your company's USP is like Ace Hardware's: "Ace is the place with the helpful hardware people." Teach consumers exactly *why* you're the best, most helpful hardware source in town.

If your company doesn't have specific reasons for being in business, then consumers will likely choose their lowest-priced option. If your company is losing business to discounters or price-oriented companies, it's even more imperative to distinguish it with a reason other than price.

Asking "Why do you do business with our store or company?" and "If you do business elsewhere, why?" of twenty-five or fifty former and current customers will give you a good start on determining your USP. Try to be as specific as possible. Go beyond just service, quality, and price because everyone claims these advantages.

Implementation

The reason this strategy is first is simple. If your business does not have a USP, it won't be in business very long; customers will not remain loyal, and your competition will beat you. Further, a well-defined and promoted USP both within the company as well as in external marketing will keep employees motivated and excited to come to work. They will know why they come in each day and will feel truly a part of the company. They will not only be better employees, but better salespeople, regardless of position.

Step One: Hold a staff meeting. Involve as many people as you can from each department in the company. Bring in your top salespeople. Invite those in production, employee administration, customer service, and management. Your objective in this staff meeting is to get the perspective of each of these departments regarding the company's USP. There will likely be different points of view and that's great. The objective is not to pass judgment or criticize any opinion. Listen to them all. Following is a sample questionnaire you can use in conducting this session.

USP Questionnaire—Owner and Staff

1. Is there owner expertise here? Credentials? Special awards?

2. Does time in business translate into unique abilities in areas of:

   - Production?
   - Delivery?
   - Product line?
   - Product quality?
   - Pricing?

3. Does any staff member have unique abilities?

4. What has been the marketing message to date? Is the USP specific? Evident in headlines?

5. Is there uniqueness in:

   - Price? *(Low price leader? Why?)*
   - Quality *(Quality better than competition? Why?)*
   - Selection *(Larger, broader selection? Be specific in types, colors, styles, quantities, etc.)*

6. Is our guarantee better than the competition's? If so, is it promoted? Can we guarantee it by a USP?

7. Does our company make it easier for the customer to do business than the competition? How?

   - More education/teaching
   - Free consultations

15

- Bonuses

- Incentives

- Better terms

- Longer hours

- Better customer service and follow-up

- Preferred customer club

- Guarantee or return policy

8. Is customer service better than the competition's? How?

- More value-added service

- Volume discount pricing

- Unique system for resolving customer complaints

- More education and more long-term relationships with customers

Step Two: Get the perspective of your customers. You want to see whether the perspective of the customer is close to that of the owners and staff. Compile a list of fifteen to twenty past customers and fifteen to twenty current customers to call, or interview customers/clients coming into the business. Explain that you're doing a brief marketing survey (or customer service follow-up) and that you're not selling anything. After a good sample of customer opinions, you'll begin to get a clear idea of the customer's perspective. Following is a sample survey with possible questions.

USP Questionnaire—Customer Version

1. Are you satisfied with the service you have received from us?

   _____

   _____

2. Is there anything you would like to see us adjust or change to serve you better?

   _____

   _____

3. What was it that caused you to choose us?

   _____

   _____

4. Have you patronized any other businesses in this industry? If yes, why?

   _____

   _____

5. Is there a crucial or obvious need that is overlooked and not being taken care of by anyone in this business?

   _____

   _____

6. What would you say is unique or that separates us from other such businesses?

   _____

   _____

Step Three: Analyze your competition. Your objective here is to determine whether the USP you are formulating really is unique. If every other competitor or even one of them is doing the same thing, then you don't have a USP.

You can survey the competition in a variety of ways:

- Shop their business (go in or call on the phone).

- Follow their advertising.

- Read all their brochures or company promotion pieces.

- Talk to their customers.

Obviously you'll need to do some of this "undercover," or perhaps ask someone outside your company to do it for you. This survey doesn't have to be totally scientific. You simply want to know what your major competitors offer and what "void" in the industry is available for your company to fill. Look for ways to differentiate your company from the competition. If a USP seems clear from your staff meeting and customer calls, then your research of the competition can be simplified by focusing on the areas suggested by staff and customers.

Following is a matrix chart to help you organize your research.

	Your Company	Competition A	Competition B	Competition C	Competition D	Competition E
Price						
Quality						
Service						
Selection						
Expertise						
Terms						
Guarantee						
Other _____						
Other _____						

Step Four: Write up your USP in ninety words or less. It will become the foundation of all your marketing. Following is a sample USP write-up:

Why Bowl at Mountain View Bowling Center?

When you bowl at Mountain View, you not only enjoy all the usual aspects of bowling, you also receive additional unique benefits, such as:

- *Open Play Club.* At Mountain View, we've rewarded the non-league bowler with an Open Play Club, a league in and of itself. The Club rewards those who would like to bowl often but not join an organized league.

- *Largest Open Play Club in the Area.* Your Open Play Club membership is not only accepted at Mountain View but also at Olympus Lanes, making the Club the largest in the area with more lanes to bowl than any other bowling center . . . fifty lanes compared to twenty or thirty. This means you'll be able to go and play without waiting as long for league bowlers to finish.

With a well-defined and articulated USP, you're ready to sell as well as launch the other marketing strategies discussed in this book. This first strategy is more involved than many of the others because it's the most critical. Without a good USP, all the other strategies would not be as effective. A good USP helps in all three ways to grow the business. It will help attract more prospects, help salespeople convert more prospects into customers, and give customers a reason to return more often and buy more, increasing customer value.

Remember—the USP should be as specific as possible. Quantify it where applicable. If your business has the best selection, for example, then the USP should describe *how* much more you have. If no USP emerges from your discussions with staff and customers, then you need to create one, perhaps by providing extra value for the same price.

Following is another example: an extra value USP for a baby boutique store. (It has been expanded beyond ninety words to be used in a promotional piece.)

The Baby Store
Extra Value Services

1. *Free delivery and set-up of cribs.* Purchase any one of the fine line of cribs available from The Baby Store, and we'll deliver and set up the crib free of charge.

2. *Gift registry.* A new/prospective mother can list her name in the gift registry at The Baby Store. She can then invite friends and family to purchase items at The Baby Store from the registry listing for showers, birthdays, or other occasions.

3. *Preferred Customer/Frequent Buyer Card.* A customer of The Baby Store can accumulate purchases of $300 and then receive a $30 gift certificate. This is our way of thanking our customers for purchasing from The Baby Store and encouraging them to come back as often as possible.

4. *Customer-base mailing list.* The Baby Store maintains and improves, each day, customer information from each customer purchase. We stay in touch with customers through phone calls and special offerings from time to time. Customers will receive information about new products they might have interest in.

5. *Gift wrapping.* The Baby Store employees are happy to gift wrap any purchase.

6. *Parent Planning Guide.* The Baby Store maintains, as a service to first-time mothers, a guide that can tell them all the things they might need in furniture as well as safety and other accessory items for the comfort of their new baby.

It is these efforts to educate, stay in touch with customers, and provide extra value that distinguishes The Baby Store from other baby furniture stores.

These extra value services become the unique selling advantages of The Baby Store.

Strategy 1
Implementation Checklist

☐ Conduct an owner and staff focus meeting.

☐ Determine unique quality points:

- Price

- Service

- Selection

- Other

☐ Survey customers.

☐ Analyze the competition.

☐ Formulate the USP into ninety words or less.

Integrating the USP

Overview

Once you have determined your unique selling proposition, it will become the overriding theme you carry into the other twenty-four strategies in this book. It's the message that should be written on invoices, work orders, and receipts. It should be communicated by all company employees. Whenever they're talking on the phone or servicing a customer, these themes should be explained.

Your USP is the focus of all radio and newspaper ads, the theme of every cross-promotion or newsletter. It should appear on any specialty advertising items—pencils, pens, refrigerator magnets—as well as on your letterhead and business cards. Benefits of the USP can become headlines for all advertising, and salespeople should incorporate it into all their sales presentations.

The USP will evolve and change as your business (and the marketplace) does. Domino's, for example, has abandoned its "thirty-minute delivery" USP because other pizza companies now can deliver in the same amount of time. As you develop an effective USP and integrate it successfully, more people will be attracted to your business. More prospects will become customers. Your customers will remain more loyal.

Implementation

You want the integration of the USP to accomplish one primary objective:

Increase the conversion rate of prospects to customers or clients.

Don't be concerned yet with increasing the number of prospects—that's accomplished with strategies discussed later. In this strategy, you want to do the best you can to determine one critical ratio: conversion rate of prospects to customers. This is often referred to as the *closing rate.*

A closing rate occurs in every type of business, regardless of industry. A professional, for example, does a certain amount of marketing and from that generates prospects. He or she should know who those prospects are and how many are becoming clients. A retail store should track the number of people coming in and then the number of transactions that occur. This can be computed to a conversion rate or closing rate. Certainly if your company has an outside sales force, you're likely tracking a closing rate.

A minimal increase in this ratio can mean a significant increase in your business's profitability. For example, consider a medical practitioner in the diet business. This doctor had prospects calling on the phone after reading his yellow pages ad, but he did not know how many of them were coming in for appointments. He started keeping track of names and addresses and sent information out to those interested. Follow-up calls were made and appointments set. This one activity alone increased business by 25 percent. However, the important thing is to understand the *profitability* increase. The doctor was already paying for the yellow pages ad, the same amount regardless of response. With a 25 percent improvement in the conversion of prospects to clients and no accompanying increase in expense, most of the increase could go right to the bottom-line profit of the practice. This is what's meant by leverage or optimization of marketing assets. In both the follow-up phone calls and the information sent, the doctor's USP was clearly presented. Before determining a USP, the doctor would not have known what to present and sell in the printed information or over the phone.

This strategy of integrating the USP applies to any marketing effort. A direct mail program that's now converting a certain percentage of prospects to clients can be improved and leveraged by integrating a good USP to improve the response. A tax professional was sending an annual mailing to people moving into her area. By integrating a USP into the mailing, response doubled. Again, there was no increase in expense—the same postage and same envelope but a different letter meant the difference. All the increase went to profit. This further illustrates leverage or optimization of marketing assets.

On the next page is a sample of a USP integrated into brochure copy for an office systems company.

XYZ Systems puts over 17 years of combined experience to work for you as we custom build the exact workstation, conference table, or round table you need in your business or home!

TRUE CUSTOM BUILT

Workstations, conference tables, round tables, and even smaller special applications are uniquely available at **XYZ SYSTEMS.**

This means that:

1. XYZ skillfully measures and builds your order to the precise size you need. The alternatives come presized in a box or are available in 6-inch increments only.

2. XYZ offers 200 color choices—you pick that "just right" color you could not find elsewhere.

3. You won't pay for what you don't need!

4. You get great looks and a perfect fit!

FAST, ON-TIME DELIVERY

This means 2 to 3 weeks from your order to our installation! XYZ delivers more than twice as fast as the "name brand" stores. Time is money—XYZ will save you 2 to 3 weeks of precious time!

AFFORDABLE PRICES FOR TOP-OF-THE-LINE QUALITY

About half the price you'd pay for high-end furnishings, and surprisingly competitive with the discount, off-the-shelf, you-put-together, in-a-box options.

XYZ Systems quality means
10-YEAR LIMITED WARRANTY!

- Special horizontal supports prevent any sagging.

- Metal slides give you quiet, easy-to-open drawers.

- Drawer frames are built for easy operation.

- 1-3/16-inch work surfaces mean years and years of durability.

- Our mobile pedestals use heavy-duty casters and let you effortlessly move them as you desire.

JOIN WITH:
Reference
Reference
and
Reference
Invite
XYZ SYSTEMS
To be of service today!

Step One: Identify all current marketing processes and implement a plan for capturing customer information. Your business or company has some sales process going on or it wouldn't be in business. It might be media advertising to bring in prospects or outside salespeople making cold calls and getting referrals. It might be a direct mail program or telemarketing effort. A manufacturer could generate leads by being on a bid list. You first need to identify all the different sales processes going on in your company. The more the better; this means more opportunity to leverage and optimize. If you don't know the conversion rate of these sales processes, then take time to track the process and record the information—plus the customer's name, address, phone, and (where possible) the amount of the purchase and for what product or service. Though other information can be captured, this should be the minimum.

The key objective in this strategy is to increase the conversion rate of prospects to customers. Integration of the USP into all selling processes will help accomplish this objective. Make certain the USP gets integrated into phone scripts, follow-up calls, and presentations. The USP gives salespeople a clear reason for selling. They will be more motivated to make more calls.

It's very important to track the current closing or conversion rate of your salespeople. Make certain that prospects contacted, presentations given, and the number of prospects converted to customers is a required report.

Remember, however, that a company can't simply hire salespeople, expect them to report progress, and hope all goes well. The enterprise must commit to train them on a regular basis.

Salespeople need to be trained in the psychology of selling. They need to know how to build trust and rapport, to probe to isolate the needs and wants of prospects. They need to know how to present their company's USP and products and services in a persuasive way. They need to know how to close a sale. They should have a follow-up system to track prospects and a system of recontacting them. They should know how to ask questions, overcome objections, and ask for the order.

It is reasonable to expect accountability from salespeople if the company builds their competence with regular sales training. By tracking and working to improve a salesperson's closing ratio, management is also managing by activity, not personality. Goals can be set and accountability related to the goals. This helps management avoid conflict and involves the salesperson in the process.

Step Two: Implement follow-up systems. One of the quickest ways to increase the closing or conversion rate of prospects to customers is by implementing a *follow-up system*. One of the best tools for follow-up is the phone. This often costs little or no money, and most sales representatives have slow time they could fill in this way.

Or perhaps a letter and a follow-up phone call works better for your product or service. For example, a moving and storage company sent a letter to all prospects worth over $500. The letter simply reaffirmed the USP and invited the prospect to call and book a date for the move. This increased the closing rate 30 percent for the company. Follow-up works well for two reasons:

- **Your competition is probably not doing it.** In other words, your company becomes even more unique by implementing follow-up systems.

- **Life, and commerce, is a moving parade.** Just because someone says "no" today doesn't mean he or she will tomorrow, next week, or even next month. Persistent follow-up can give your sales force a chance to resell the prospect over and over, helping prospective customers decide to do business with your company.

The follow-up may even require a personal visit. The nature or extent of your follow-up can be determined by the potential sale amount. Deciding when to follow up will depend on the buying cycle and habits of your customers. While a computer company may know that people make a decision to buy a computer within twenty-four and seventy-two hours, another type of business may have a two-week window of receptivity to follow up. Create your system around this cycle.

Not only will a good follow-up system help increase the conversion rate, it will improve and build upon customer service. Your customers will become more endeared to your company. They will be more loyal and respond to invitations to return and do business. People love to be led and nurtured in the buying process.

Following is a sample format for tracking the productivity of inside salespeople.

Salesperson's Name				Month					Year	
Day	Total Sales	Total # of Items	Total # of Sales	Avg $ Per Sale	Avg $ Per Item	Avg Item Per Sale	Total Hours	Avg $ Per Hour		
1										
2										
3										
4										
5										
6										
7										
8										
9										
10										
11										
12										
13										
14										
15										
16										
17										
18										

Day	Total Sales	Total # of Items	Total # of Sales	Avg $ Per Sale	Avg $ Per Item	Avg Item Per Sale	Total Hours	Avg $ Per Hour		
19										
20										
21										
22										
23										
24										
25										
26										
27										
28										
29										
30										
31										

Strategy 2
Implementation Checklist

☐ Identify all areas of selling in your company: phone, ads, salespeople, mailings, brochures, and so on.

☐ Integrate the USP into marketing activity:

- Headlines

- Ads

- Sales presentations

- Phone scripting

- Mailings

☐ Track and record closing rates.

☐ Implement follow-up systems.

☐ Evaluate any changes in response from prospects (e.g., closing rate increase, etc.).

Databasing Past Customers

Overview

Nine out of ten businesses do not capture the names of all the customers and prospects coming into their place of operation. Businesses seem to watch prospects come in, turn around, and walk out, despite having invested thousands of dollars in overhead expenses, salaries, utilities, advertising, and perhaps years of goodwill, to get those people to come in.

The prospects coming in are doing so for a reason. They have a need or want, or a problem to be solved. The company has *paid for* this prospect. Therefore, it's important to get the names, addresses, and phone numbers of all customers and prospects and keep them on file. If you work in a professional office, then the name of every person who inquires by phone or comes in for a quote on your services should be recorded. Besides names, addresses, and phone numbers, capture as much other information as you can. Find out what products or services the person was interested in or what they purchased. Record how much he or she spent.

Information about customers and prospects can be captured on a simple 3 x 5 card by entering them in a drawing or sweepstakes. Your company might give away a free television, blanket, or luggage—perhaps a free consultation. Have the customer fill out information on a card and place it in a box for a free drawing. Ask for the customer's name, address, phone number, and how he or she heard about your service or company. Include any other information you feel would be helpful. Put this information into a computer database. Databased marketing is the wave of the future.

One store had traffic of nearly three hundred people a day, but for twelve years had never captured customer information. In a week, that company would have had eighteen hundred names or so on file or six to seven thousand names a month. True, some of these would be duplicates, but they could easily be purged. Such a file on the computer can track repeat customers and how many times they are coming in and how much they're spending.

One strategy that can be very effective for quickly increasing sales and profits is to invite past customers to return and do business with your company. Many times a company will become so involved in keeping up with current purchases and current business that they forget past customers. It's been proven that nearly 65 percent of customers stop doing business with a company because of the apathy they perceive from the owner and/or staff. Over time, they become resentful for giving so much to the business yet apparently getting nothing back in return. And if they feel neglected, they will switch to another company that offers the same product or service for less money.

A big reason many companies neglect past customers is because they don't know what to talk to them about. Now you do—your USP, your unique selling proposition. Be straightforward: Admit you've neglected them, and ask them to come back. Give them a special offer. Help them understand your unique position in the marketplace.

Do a test. Choose a few hundred or even a thousand past customers who have not made a purchase in a year and contact them, perhaps with just a phone call. Besides stimulating sales, this will also help you clean up your customer list and delete those who have moved and left the area. A doctor in the weight control business had five hundred past customers. One letter inviting them back drew in 125 of them, increasing his business 25 percent in just thirty days!

Don't forget past customers. With the right offer and approach, you may get them back.

Implementation

Step One: Capturing customer information. If your company has not been documenting customer information—start now. Many point-of-sale systems can capture names, addresses, phone numbers, and other pertinent data. They can also tell how often a customer makes a purchase and how much he or she spends. They can track what colors the customer likes, important dates for the customer to remember, and so on.

If your company has such information, begin implementing this strategy by segmenting the customers into Past, Present, and Prospective. Many times past customer records are discarded—don't let your company make this mistake! If customers stop doing business with your company, you want to know why. Among other things, it can help your company make changes to the USP. It can help reveal policies that get in the way of customers doing more business with you. You might learn of personality problems with staff or salespeople. In other words, working with past customers is a great marketing research opportunity. But, beyond that opportunity, it extends an opportunity to make more profit. Gather the records that define what a past customer is for your business. Again, depending on the buying cycle, a past customer may be defined as someone who hasn't purchased in a month or even a year.

Step Two: Set up a system of communicating with past customers. The sales staff, sales clerks, or administrative personnel can be assigned fifty to one hundred of the top past customers to contact and invite back to the business. Those doing the contacting don't need to be telemarketing experts. This isn't a sales call (although this will often be the result); it's simply an invitation for past customers to come back and shop again. The approach can be something as simple as the following:

Hello, Mrs. Brown. My name is Susan with XYZ Company. We just wanted to let you know how much we have appreciated having you as a customer. This is advance notice about a special we are having next week. (Then describe the special.) *We invite you into the store to take advantage of the special this week before we let the general public know. Again, thanks for doing business with us. We hope to see you again soon. If there is anything else we might help you with, please let us know. Thank you and good-bye.*

The remaining past customers can be contacted by mail. The reason to start with top customers is so you can test the response to certain offers. Those offers that are successful can be used in the general mailing.

Step Three: Conduct some mailings. In trying to bring back past customers to your business, you can test by doing regular mailings making different offers. In these mailings, it's critical to include certain elements. Highlight your USP with a headline (for example, a USP or slogan like "Fresh Mexican food in under two minutes" easily can become a headline). Be straightforward. Explain your rationale for inviting them back and be up-front about the offer. To illustrate, one business owner in the automobile service industry was being forced to move from his location and needed ten thousand dollars to do so. He didn't have the money, but he did have a big marketing asset in five hundred past customers. He wrote them a letter, explaining he was being forced to relocate and to cover the costs would provide five hundred dollar's worth of service over the next year if the customer would prepurchase it for three hundred dollars now. He raised the ten thousand dollars.

Step Four: Test your market. Successful implementation of any marketing strategy may not happen on the first try. Even the best marketing consultants will explain that the marketplace is the only true judge of any offer or marketing approach. Many business owners are so convinced that their customers or prospects will love an offer (and all of them will buy) that they make the mistake of sending out one offer to the whole list. A business manager for an artist sent out 25,000 mail pieces to art museums around the country at a total cost of forty thousand dollars. He did not receive one order. Don't make this mistake. The man should have tested a few thousand pieces and listened to the response of his market. He could have then tried four or five other offers, different letter copy, and different pricing. This would have given his target market a chance to respond to the offer they most wanted. Then he could send out more mailings with the best offer. His chances for success would have been greatly multiplied.

In your testing, be sure to test only one variable at a time. That way, you'll better know which part of your approach worked. For example, change the price and keep everything else the same. Then, change the offer or the headline.

Be patient. Don't give up the effort to recapture past customers if they didn't respond immediately to one certain offer. Try again. Test in small quantities before you roll out a big campaign. This is another good reason to test by phone before you mail. On the other hand, past customers are going to need more selling, so several tests will probably be required. But the return is exciting. Marketing more to past customers helps you grow the business by increasing customer value or worth. You can win customers back and keep them coming back as you integrate your USP and test on a regular basis.

Following is a reactivation letter that worked very well for a diet doctor.

YOUR NEW BEGINNING BEFORE THE HOLIDAYS!
You can lose 10-40 pounds in the next 8 weeks
safely and without feeling hungry.
Plus . . .
you'll feel well and healthy for good!

Dear _____

It's been a while since we worked with you to help you lose weight and feel a return to full health. We hope things are going well for you.

If things aren't going well, we'd like to offer some help. Being overweight can hurt more than just your looks. According to the National Institute of Health, obesity is, in fact, a disease with serious risks and consequences. If you are overweight currently, you increase your risk of developing one or more of the following:

- Gall bladder disease

- High blood pressure

- Endometrial cancer

- Diabetes mellitus

- Osteoarthritis

Obesity can even exert its worst effect on your sense of self-esteem. It creates an enormous psychological burden. In fact, in terms of suffering, this burden may even be the greatest adverse effect of being overweight.

If you did it before, you can do it again, and

we're better prepared to help you keep it off for good!

We know that some of you may have gained your weight back and may be experiencing symptoms of medical consequence. You lost the weight before but may be feeling you can't do it again. Or, you don't want to experience the weight loss only to gain it back. We understand.

There are several new benefits available to you, a former patient with the XYZ Group, that can help you lose the weight more comfortably and keep it off for good!

We have now expanded our product line to include great-tasting dinner entrees. The beef, chicken, and pasta selections are low-calorie, nutritionally balanced entrees to complement the effective use of our shakes.

With this approach, you'll lose the weight fast . . . 3 to 5 pounds a week. And, you'll do it safely, with balanced nutrition.

If, on the other hand, you want a more gradual weight loss program, we are having great success with our "Be Your Best" program. Our shakes, cookies, and cereals, along with vitamins and, at your option, 8 to 12 injections, have helped many people successfully lose weight. This program is especially effective if you only need to shed 15 pounds or so.

There's also our low-calorie self-diet program. We'll help you plan a low-calorie menu and then, with a doctor's supervision, stay on it. We'll help you see that you maintain adequate nutrition.

Get started now before the holidays and save 50%.

Some of you on a previous program may not need a complete work-up. If that's the case, we'll give you 50% off any tests or exams you might need to get started.

If a full work-up is required, we'll still give you a 50% discount at $130. But if you have insurance, it could cover much of the cost and get you started almost for free!

How we're better prepared to help you keep it off—for good!

If you're ready to lose the weight and return to full health, call our office at 123-4567. Jane Doe has joined the staff at XYZ Group full time for one reason—to help you stay on the plan you choose and help you change your eating habits for good. And she's well qualified. Besides her professional training, she lost over 30 pounds with XYZ Product and has kept it off. She's here to talk to when you get discouraged and to listen when we need to improve our patient relations.

And, she'll help you choose a plan that best fits your budget. All three programs—XYZ Products, "Be Your Best," and low-calorie self-dieter—have different cost schedules. Jane can help you move from one plan to another as your needs change.

There's a bonus if you restart by October 31!

If you're really serious about losing pounds, keeping them off, and returning to full health and well-being, we're more serious than ever about helping you. We have contracted with a phone service and are beginning to record support messages. This means that whenever you are discouraged or tempted to "cheat," you can call and hear an affirming message for that day or week.

This special service will be available at no charge to you if you restart by October 31. Call at your leisure. Call at night. Call in the morning. Call from work. Call from bed. Call and receive the encouragement you might need at a weak moment to continue your diet and reach your goals.

Call now—123-4567—and ask for Jane. Schedule your appointment today. Let us help you lose weight before the holidays and keep it off for good.

Sincerely,

Philip Doctor, M.D.

P.S. Lose 8 to 40 pounds in the next 8 weeks. 50% off the cost of restarting. New additions to diet programs. New on-staff support and a bonus—start by October 31 and join a support message network—free.

Strategy 3
Implementation Checklist

☐ Implement methods of capturing customer information.

☐ Identify past customers.

☐ Invite them back (USP).

☐ Test different offers.

Communicating With Current Customers

Overview

After capturing information about your customers, communicate with them on a regular basis. Don't worry about being a marketing expert to communicate the right way. As a rule, you don't need elaborate direct mail schemes with sizzling headlines, awesome copy, and irresistible offers. Just extend a simple invitation to your customer to come back and do business. The results from such an approach will certainly be worth the effort.

For example, Mr. Brown brings his car into your repair service for a state license-renewal inspection. The trained technician observes that even though the automobile passes the inspection criteria, there's wear on the brakes and a damaged muffler. He draws Mr. Brown's attention to this and recommends future service. This information can then be put into the repair shop computer with the command to alert the operator a month from now to call that customer and invite him back for brake or muffler work. This is communicating one-on-one.

When Mrs. Brown visits a local boutique and purchases a pair of shoes, this information is recorded. Later that month, as the salesclerk is doing markdowns, she calls Mrs. Brown about a particular outfit and explains how nice it would look with the new pair of shoes. She invites Mrs. Brown to come in and take a look. This is personal marketing.

Customer communications can coincide with any sales or promotions the business is offering. They can be the same invitations that the newspaper or radio is making. They can be invitations that coincide with a birthday or holiday. One department store with a tire center made a special offer to customers during the winter months for tires. Clerks and salespeople were invited to call their regular customers back with a special tire service offer. This invitation is not a telemarketing sales pitch. It's simply an invitation that goes like this:

Hello, Mr. Smith. This is Bill with XYZ Company. I noticed you were in last month and purchased a blazer. I wanted to let you know we just received some good-looking shirts and sweaters that would look great with your coat. I wanted to invite you to take advantage of the terrific selection we have now. Thank you for shopping with us!

For a more fine-tuned approach, go through your customer base and identify the top 20 percent who do business with you on a regular basis. These are the ones that need to be rewarded consistently or they'll begin doing business elsewhere. Perhaps issue a card that identifies them as a preferred customer and provides them important discounts or extra service on certain products. These good customers need to be recognized and rewarded if they're going to repeat their behavior.

The types of rewards you offer can vary. It might be a 10 percent discount on a special outfit that's going on sale that month. It might be a new tie that goes with the purchase of a new jacket. It might be an invitation to join the preferred customer club. The incentive does not need to be costly, but simply an indication to these customers that they're needed. They in turn will feel good about your company and tell others. Because new customers will be attracted by the policy, it can be a USP by itself.

You can easily measure the results of this marketing strategy. Record customer information and put it into a database or card filing system. If you develop an invitation or letter to invite these people back to do business, simply ask them to bring the letter back to the store. You can measure the response to your offer as well as the additional sales the idea generated.

Implementation

One of your company's greatest marketing assets is your current customers. However, many business owners and managers fail to see the leverage and optimization opportunities with current customers. The objective with this strategy is the same as with past customers—increasing customer value or worth. You want to have current customers buying from you more often and, at the same time, buying more at each transaction.

Step One: Capture customer information. As discussed, make certain your company is capturing all the information it can about customers.

Step Two: Identify back-end and cross-selling opportunities both within and outside your company. After tracking customers' first-time buying habits, begin listing complementary products and services that relate to that first purchase. It is these products and services that become back-end selling. When you buy a car, have you noticed how the dealer will offer you warranties, accessories, financing options, insurance, and other products that relate to your purchase? The tape and CD clubs let first-time buyers select multiple tapes for a penny because they know on the back end they will have club members for life buying tapes at the regular price. A CPA might start a client with bookkeeping services but then back-end for quarterly and annual reports or tax service. You want to be certain to make follow-up offers after a customer's initial purchase; however, the products or services don't always have to be complementary.

The important principle in this strategy is to understand that what the customer purchased is less important than your relationship with him or her. It's this relationship that's the asset, not the purchase. This means your company should also be cross-selling all products and services. If a CPA firm also employs attorneys in the office, these services should be marketed to clients using the CPA service. A retail store that sells adult clothing but also carries children's wear should invite adult customers to come in and shop for their children. After your company has exhausted all product and service offers within the company, relationships with other businesses can provide more selling opportunities and more chances to increase customer value or worth. A real estate agent should establish relationships with landscapers, furniture stores, and security firms and offer the products or services of these companies to home buyers.

Step Three: Set up a system of communicating with current customers. Just as you need a system of communicating with past customers, you need one to communicate with current ones. It's important to understand you want more than just a mailing list that you use to send offers once or twice a year. With back-end and cross-selling, both within and outside your company, you can see that the opportunities to ask current customers to buy again from you are great. Some business owners are concerned about offering too often and offending the recipients. That's why you must *test*. The frequency of your offers will depend on your product, complementary products, and your customers' buying frequency.

Remember, don't stop communicating with your customers just because you think you've probably done enough. Your customers will tell you how often by their response rate. If a mailing and offer prove profitable, do it again. Declining response will let you know the frequency with which you should contact your customers. Offers to current customers can also be made by phone as well as mail, or a combination. It's also a good idea to assign the top 20 percent of your clientele to your top salespeople. Make it a required part of their ongoing sales effort to communicate with current customers and treat them as preferred buyers. A preferred customer club provides a great way to communicate with current customers, perhaps using a newsletter. Some companies outsource their customer service follow-up.

However you choose to communicate, the overture is very important not only to boost sales, but also for the customer service value alone. If people feel they are important to your company, they'll remain loyal. They'll also be more likely to return again and again. Remember, 65 percent of people stop doing business with a company because of a feeling of apathy they get from staff, management, and owners. So as a minimum, your communication system in this strategy should be for customer service follow-up. But then work to expand the offers you make. The value of your customers to your business will increase through repeat purchasing opportunities.

Step Four: Increase the value of each purchase. In working with current customers, you not only want them to buy more often, you want them to buy more with each purchase. You don't want to be pushy or try to sell people things they don't want. However, with proper training, salespeople can learn professional techniques to help people buy more. This can be done by upselling (to be discussed in detail in Strategy 8) and packaging, which involves bundling related products and services to help increase the average sale of each purchase. You can see how the fast food industry has done this with combo meals and "supersizing." Just follow that example. Again, list the complementary products and services you have and package them. Test your package with current customers and perhaps give them a discount. Make certain that salespeople are trained to find out all the needs and wants of customers. Then they should know how to professionally meet these through upselling and packaging.

Following is an example of a heating and air conditioning company's letter to current customers. It invites them to prepare their cooling systems for summer. Also, as part of its USP, this company formed a Comfort Plus Club.

If You Beat the Heat, You Could Save a Lot of Money!
May Is the Month

Dear Preferred Customer:

May - May - May is the month. Don't wait for the heat. It could cost you a lot in terms of money and discomfort. During the month of May, let XYZ Company

Prepare your cooling system for summer for
Only $39.95*
(*parts extra)

Then we'll winterize it in the fall—for free!
Call 123-4567 now! Offer ends May 31.

This offer includes your swamp cooler or your central air system. You'll save at least $55.00. That's $15 off our regular service fee of $54.95, and $39.95 saved on our special for winterization.

But you could save a lot more. You see, starting up your system during the demands of heat in June or failing to winterize your system in the fall can put severe strains on the motor, wiring, etc. Parts can break under the strain, causing more damage and running up a repair bill. That's why we're happy to winterize FREE!

Your cooling system will get a complete 15-point check for only $39.95:

1. Install gauges and check operating pressures.

2. Check voltage and amperage to all motors with meter.

3. Check air temperature drop across evaporator.

4. Check for adequate refrigerant charge and possible leaks.

5. Check evaporator superheat.

6. Lubricate all moving parts.

7. Check belt and adjust tension.

8. Check filters.

9. Check pressure switch cut-out settings.

10. Check electrical lock out circuits.

11. Check starting contractor contacts.

12. Check all wiring and connections.

13. Clean and adjust thermostat.

14. Check air temperature across condenser.

15. Check that condensation drain is open. Turn exposed dampers to cooling position, if marked (no balancing).

But, please do it in May. When summer starts, we're busy servicing and repairing air conditioning systems. Give us a call before things heat up.

Thank you,

John Doe

P.S. Call now—123-4567. We'll prepare your cooling system for summer for only $39.95. Save at least $55 and maybe a lot more! We'll then winterize your system in the fall—FREE!

Your Private Invitation to Join

The New Comfort Plus Club and Enjoy

Comfort • Safety • Peace of Mind • Better Health

And . . . Lower Utility Bills 365 Days a Year!

Special Introductory Offer for AAA Customers Only!

Register by March 31

Dear Preferred Customer:

Enclosed is information about our new AAA Comfort Plus Club, an exclusive heating and air conditioning maintenance service plan that we want to offer first to our current customers at a *low introductory price.*

The brochure explains how you can have your furnace, air conditioning unit, and water heater serviced and repaired 365 days a year at one low annual membership fee.

At AAA Company, we have watched the cost of maintaining appliances and the costs of utility service increase dramatically during the 15 years we have serviced customers in Utah Valley. We're sure you've noticed also. We want to help you lower these costs. We know if you take advantage of this introductory offer to join our Comfort Plus Club, you will realize tremendous savings. In the brochure, you'll learn how your membership could easily pay for itself in one service call or repair!

You'll also learn how your membership will help you live more comfortably in the summer and winter with increased safety, peace of mind, and better health.

After you've read about your membership benefits, fill out the attached membership registration card and mail it back to AAA Company by March 31 to secure your membership at this low introductory price. We'll get you enrolled and begin setting aside time for your FREE service check on your air conditioning unit before the spring rush hits in April.

Thanks for your loyalty as an AAA Company customer. We hope this new club membership will be another way we can continue serving you for years to come.

Sincerely,

John Doe

P.S. Read the enclosed brochure and learn now how you can save money and enjoy greater comfort, safety, peace of mind, and health all year long. Our new club will bring you all these benefits upon your enrollment.

Strategy 4
Implementation Checklist

- ☐ Implement a method for capturing customers.
- ☐ Identify current customers.
- ☐ Identify other products/services you could sell.
- ☐ Determine an offer.
- ☐ Test, using mail, phone, or a combination.

Identifying Prospective Customers

Overview

One of the very important concepts that businesses lose sight of is the idea of the moving parade. Even though prospects may not immediately take advantage of what you have to offer, one day something may take place that changes their situation and necessitates your product or service. This is the idea of the moving parade. People's needs change day by day. This possible gold mine awaits in unconverted prospects or leads.

Each day people call to inquire about your company's products or mail in for information. Ten to thirty percent become customers. What about the other 70 to 90 percent? If they inquired or if they came into the store, it must have been because of a particular need or want. Perhaps because the price was out of range or the person who helped them was incompetent, they simply decided to postpone their decision. With a follow-up effort, either through the mail or on the phone, you might catch them as their needs and situations change.

Your approach in the mail or over the phone could be something like, "Hi, my name is John Smith with XYZ Company. We noticed that you came and visited our firm this past month and wanted to follow up to see if we could be of help to you." A simple invitation to do business.

Whenever the company attends trade shows or has a booth, make sure to capture names. Don't make the mistake of discarding the names after the Marketing Department has made contact. If that happens, no follow-up can occur.

Implementation

Step One: Capture prospect information. As with current and past customers, make certain your company is capturing prospect information. The people who inquire about your product or service and the leads your organization's salespeople generate form the basis of your list of prospective customers.

Many excellent software tools (called *contact managers*) are available to capture and track prospective customers. These software applications allow you to determine a schedule for recontacting prospects and how you will do so—phone, mail, fax, or even in person. Your tracking information might include, beyond name, address and phone, what the prospect was interested in, the dollar range in which he or she wants to spend, and when the prospect may be most likely to buy.

Step Two: Set up your follow-up system. Just as with past and current customers, you need to determine how and when follow-up will occur with prospects. Prospects who aren't going to be followed up with by salespeople can be contacted through a company mailing or telemarketing system.

A simple follow-up form or card such as the one that follows can be made to help with the day-to-day capturing of prospect information.

Follow-up Card

Name _____

Address _____

Phone_____

Fax_____

Date _____

Products/Services Interested In:

_____

_____

_____

Follow-up Date_____

$ Amount _____

The reason an amount is included is to help you qualify which prospects might be the most likely to buy and are considering the most profitable purchases. These prospects would be a priority in follow-up efforts. For example, a retail store may not want to follow up with any prospects under $50. This can help you keep your salespeople paying attention to the most lucrative prospects.

Step Three: Find another use for prospect names. Many times, through the sales process, your company will generate prospects who are not really qualified for your product or service. They may be in the wrong demographic group or may not be able to afford your product. In this situation, make a deal with another company, even in your same industry, to sell these leads or exchange the names for prospects who may better fit your company's customer profile. Remember, the gathering of prospects is a marketing asset you want to leverage and optimize to the fullest. So, in this case, even a competitor may be a source of revenue for you without damaging your competitive position, because the prospect doesn't fit your company's profile anyway!

You can also turn this around. If your company is fairly new and does not yet have the marketing budget to generate fresh prospects, look for a similar situation with another company in your industry. Agree to pay that company a fee for the names or exchange them for other value your company could provide. This is a way you can build your company's prospect pool without spending an extra dime on advertising.

Step Four: Test. Try different approaches with prospects just as you should with past and current customers.

Strategy 5
Implementation Checklist

- [ ] Implement a system to capture prospect names, addresses, and phone numbers.

- [ ] Determine the best tool for follow-up:

  - Phone

  - Letter

  - Newsletter

  - Salesperson

- [ ] Determine the best timing for follow-up.

- [ ] Consider making a deal with another company to share leads.

- [ ] Test, evaluate, and test again.

Getting Letters of Endorsement

Overview

Your company can generate new customers through previous and current customers by way of letters of endorsement.

For example, go through your database and choose the top ten customers who also have client or customer bases that might be predisposed to buy what your company offers. Perhaps you're an insurance agent who has a client who's an auto dealer, and she in turn has a clientele of hundreds, perhaps thousands, of car buyers. If this dealer has been pleased with your services, then develop a letter with her endorsement to her customers referring your auto coverage services to them.

This is a very professional and effective way to get your customers working for your company, influencing thousands of other potential customers. It's an organized referral system. Many customers are happy to do it simply on request, though you might offer them a gift.

Here's how a letter of endorsement might read from the auto dealer to her customers in behalf of an insurance agent:

Dear Customer:

For several years I have had the opportunity of having my insurance needs handled by Bob Jones. He has been an exceptional agent with a competent understanding of the changing financial situation.

I have prevailed upon Bob to offer you a free consultation because you are one of my customers. With no charge or obligation at all, Bob will give you an overview of financial services and take an inventory of your needs.

I wanted to tell you about him and let you know I endorse his services 100%.

Please give him a call at 942-7725 to set up a time for your free consultation.

Sincerely yours,

Stella Brown

Midtown Auto Sales

This is a very simple letter of endorsement, but it can have a powerful effect. With consistent letters of endorsement going out every month from four to five happy customers, you can immediately gauge results from that letter because the offer will be specific to them as customers of the endorser.

This can also be very low cost because you could send a test mailing of fifty or one hundred letters to see the response—a minimal investment. Likewise, the letters could go out with regular billings from the endorser. Overnight, you can effectively reach thousands or more potential customers very economically through letters of endorsement. Be sure to pick customers who have complementary product lines, or those who are employees, managers, or owners of complementary businesses. That way your audience is targeted.

Implementation

Your company probably already gets a portion of new business from referrals. All you want to do in this strategy is create a proactive referral marketing system. In other words, rather than wait and hope for customers to give you referrals, this strategy of endorsements can make the referral process ongoing and a part of your overall marketing strategy.

Step One: Identify endorsement sources. First, take time to consider who currently gives your company referrals. These businesses or individuals are probably in your top 20 percent of customers in terms of how often and how much they purchase from your company. List these customers. Then as, you consider each of them, ask the question, "Does this customer or client in turn have a customer or client base who would be predisposed to buying my company's product or services?"

Step Two: Contact these customers. Approach each of these customers with the following: "Tom, you've been a valued customer of ours, and we appreciate your business very much. We want to expand our business and felt that the clients you have would probably be interested in our product/service as well. We'd like your help in reaching them. We will write the letter, pay for the postage, pay for your letterhead expense, and mail to just a small sampling of your customer base to see if they are interested in our product. Would that be workable for you?" You might even want to go to this meeting with a possible endorsement letter already written.

Most of your satisfied customers will be happy to help you build your business—they probably already have given you referrals. The key is to reassure them this will not cost them money and take any of their time. It's important to have the letter written on their letterhead and with the owner's signature. It should then be mailed out in their envelope. The mailing can be done from either your business or your customer's. Also, reassure your customer that it will be a small test. With this approach, your chance for success is greater.

Step Three: Craft the letter. The endorsement letter should contain an endorsement of your company's USP. It should then sell prospects on your USP and give them a special offer because they are customers of your client or customer.

Step Four: Test. After obtaining approval for the endorsement and crafting the letter, test a portion of the customer base. If the test works out well, it is likely your customer will then allow you to mail out more or even the remainder of the customer base. Get as many endorsements as you can. The objective of this strategy is to build your prospect pool without spending an extra dime on advertising.

Step Five: Identify other sources of endorsements. After you have attained endorsements from your in-house customer base, look outside to complementary businesses or professionals. Seek their endorsement of your product or service to their customer base. In this case, you might need to work out a different arrangement. You could exchange customer bases or pay a rental fee for the list. Endorsement letters are a very low cost yet highly leveraged marketing strategy. Make certain they are an ongoing part of your company's marketing strategy.

Strategy 6
Implementation Checklist

- ☐ List customers who currently give your company referrals.
- ☐ Identify your other top five to ten customers.
- ☐ Identify those who have customers that are likely prospects for your company.
- ☐ Craft an endorsement letter.
- ☐ Approach endorser prospects.
- ☐ Test three or four endorsement letters.
- ☐ Evaluate and change offers, and test again.

Staging Cross-Promotions

Overview

Cross-promotions are coupons or value cards placed in a complementary business establishment that has high traffic volume and is willing to make the value card available on your company's behalf.

Generally with cross-promotions, you can distribute as many cards as you want. They're also attractive in that you have some control in reaching the type of customer who would be drawn to your product or service. Further, cross-promotions fix the responsibility of the discount on the cross-promoter rather than on you. When you run a newspaper ad or coupon announcing a discount, everyone, including competitors, knows it's your company spending money to give customers a discount. But an important element of cross-promotion is that it is "compliments of." (It's very difficult for a competitor to figure out what's going on because it's a low-key, quiet marketing approach.) You can have a one-way cross-promotion, which simply involves another store distributing your promotional piece, or you can enter into a two-way promotion where you agree to distribute promotions for the other store too.

The first step is to approach the owners of the complementary businesses you identify. You might say something like:

> *Hi, I'm Susan Jones working with Platinum Clothing here in town. I have something I thought was interesting and wanted you to take a look at it.*

> *Here's how it works. I would like to offer you the opportunity to help your customers get more for their money, a way for you to say 'thank you' for shopping at your store. (Show the cross-promotion sample.)*

> *About how many people come into your store weekly? I will have printed up cross-promotion cards and bring them by for distribution to each of your customers. You will need to hand them out or put them in the sack, not just leave them on the counter. In return, I can hand out a similar card for your business. Should we go ahead and get this started?*

Though you should be able to follow this format and be successful, you might need to approach ten owners to get one to participate. You should have a target of distributing hundreds of cards weekly. You can gauge the response from these cross-promotions as people bring in the cards. Following is what a cross-promotion card might look like:

A Special Thank You

from

Platinum Clothing

ABC Hanks Blvd.

Town, Michigan

SAVE $10

on your dry cleaning

Experts Cleaning

Def Harrison Blvd.

Town, Michigan

- - - - - - - - - - - - - - - - - -

This coupon good for $10 off a $25 or more

dry cleaning order at Experts Cleaning

Expires _____

Implementation

This strategy is most effective if you have a business with a lot of customer and prospect traffic on a regular basis, such as a retail store. However, the concept can work with any business and even with professionals. Let's work through an example using a clothing retail store.

Step One: Make a list of possible cross-promotion alliances. The stores should be in the same general geographic area as your customers and should have customer demographics that are similar to those of your store. If you owned a clothing store, you could set up cross-promotions with a jewelry store, a shoe store, and perhaps a dry cleaner.

Step Two: Draw up a sample cross-promotion piece. You can do this with many computer software applications or have a graphic designer help you.

Step Three: Approach your cross-promotion alliance prospect. Simply go through the scripting provided in the Overview. Again, if you enjoy good relationships with most other nearby business owners, the response will be positive. Set up as many cross-promotions as you can service and track.

Step Four: Track results. Confirm that the cross-promotion pieces are distributed by hand—don't let them sit on the counter. Record the number of responses you get and track which alliance works most effectively.

Following are a couple more examples of cross-promotions, one with a lighting store and another with a women's lingerie store. Notice that the company's USP is on each cross-promotion piece.

Thank You from
ABC Company

Save 5% on all shades or
period pieces at

XYZ COMPANY

*Over 1,500 shade patterns, 300 fabric choices,
and 3,000 frames in stock. We create custom
shades and offer lamp and shade repair.*

100 South Main
City, State 54321
(800) 123-4567

Offer good through February 28.
One per person.

Compliments of

MMM Company

Save 10% on the purchase of

TWO tailored jackets at

regular price

Your Clothing Store

Professional fitters

helping you:

Feel better

Look better

Save money

Offer good through March 25.
One per person.
Offer good only at Downtown Mall Store.

Strategy 7
Implementation Checklist

☐ Identify other business owners with businesses that complement yours.

☐ Take a sample of a cross-promotion to the owner to examine.

☐ Make sure the owner is willing to distribute the cards and not just leave them on the counter.

☐ Match the number of promotion cards to the weekly foot traffic.

☐ Test different values for the card.

☐ Perhaps establish a special deal for the employees of the store to make certain that your cards are distributed.

☐ Include the proper disclaimers to avoid any miscommunication and violation.

Upselling

Overview

Very few companies work on the skill of upselling, yet it can be one of your most effective tools for increasing sales and profits without any increased effort or expense on your part.

After a sale is complete, offer the customer additional products and services. Every sales encounter should be maximized as far as the amount of sale or profit opportunity. Auto dealerships present a tremendous example of upselling. When you buy a car, they offer you additional products such as rust inhibitor, service warranties, insurance, and so forth. If three or four out of ten people take these additional products after the initial sale, then the average overall sale of the car is up several hundred dollars. This adds significant profit to the bottom line.

Any company can employ upselling. Salespeople at retail establishments need to regard themselves as profit centers. If they have a thousand-dollar-a-month salary, they need to bring in two or three thousand dollars a month by themselves to pay for that salary. They can do this almost entirely through upselling.

A certain hardware store's average sale was ten to twelve dollars. With three hundred people a day coming into the store, they were generating three to four thousand dollars in sales per day. To implement effective upselling opportunities, the first question floor salespeople would ask a customer coming into the store was, "What project are you working on?" They could get an idea of all of the customer's hardware needs and offer them at the time of sale. This would increase the average sale from ten to perhaps fifteen or maybe twenty dollars. These extra transactions a day can be a significant increase for a store. If the customer purchases forty dollars worth of merchandise, your salespeople could be authorized to offer an additional forty dollars at 20 to 50 percent off as an add-on to the current forty-dollar sale. If the add-on is of high perceived value, a certain percentage will take advantage of the offer. How much the upsell will add to the bottom line of your company depends on the products sold and the packages offered.

Another good example of upselling comes from lawn care services. Just prior to sending out a service technician, someone from the company calls to explain the pest control and tree service, offering to add either or both to the current service at a discount. You encounter upselling every time you visit a McDonald's or Hardee's. When you order a burger, they offer fries and a drink. When you order a burger and fries, they offer you a drink and a dessert. They are taught how to increase the size of the order by upselling. They now package these offers into "combo" meals. This same basic strategy can be used by virtually all kinds of businesses. It's one of the most neglected yet effective techniques for improving the dollar volume of every sales transaction.

Implementing the technique of upselling does not require extensive sales training. Simply design packages around products currently sold. When a customer or prospect comes in and orders a certain product, have a package identified with that request ready and offer it to the customer. The package is simply a group of products that complement the one the customer specifies. It increases the potential sale amount. For example, let's say a customer comes into a clothing store and buys a pair of shoes. The sales clerk would know there is a wardrobe also on sale that she could package around that pair of shoes and offer at a 5 to 10 percent discount. The sales clerk would simply take the customer over to the package and show her what is available—one out of five might purchase the package.

Implementation

Step One: Identify add-ons and packaging. First, make a list of items that could be bundled and grouped in packages. Then do the same for add-ons. Identify the products or services that complement the products or services customers purchase most frequently. Build your packages and add-ons around these top-selling products and services.

Step Two: Provide sales training. On the next page is a worksheet for upselling. Involve your salespeople in creating packages and add-ons. Then take them through the sheet titled "When and Where to Upsell" (customize as necessary to fit your situation). The summary sheet titled "How I Can Increase My Personal Sales Production Now" can help combine training for increasing closing rate with training to increase the average sale amount through upselling.

Learning to Upsell—The Key is Packaging

(List package possibilities)

1. _____
2. _____
3. _____
4. _____
5. _____
6. _____

Add-Ons

(List add-on products/services)

1. _____
2. _____
3. _____
4. _____
5. _____
6. _____

When and Where to Upsell

WHEN:

After the initial purchase decision

After you're sure they are owners

After 7 to 10 days (follow-up)

WHERE:

Working the floor

Putting things in their hands

Building "their pile" at the register

How I Can Increase My Personal Sales Production Now

1. Think and act in terms of customers' needs, wants, and desires.

2. Learn all I can about my products and services so I can better educate my customers.

   "The more I tell, the more I sell."

   "The more I teach, the more I'll reach."

3. Shift the mind-set from single purchases to packages and multiple sales.

4. Ask for the order.

5. Set personal productivity goals.

6. Follow up, follow up, follow up!

Step Three: Measure. To make certain the primary objective of upselling is reached—increasing the average sale amount on a customer's purchase—you need to see that your company can and does calculate and track regularly the average sale not only for the company but for individual sales representatives. This is the second way your company can increase the value or worth of each customer. When upselling and increasing the average sale is combined with increasing the number of repeat purchases, a dramatic increase in profits can be realized.

It's the measuring and accounting of these two ratios—closing and average sale—on which all sales training should focus. It's very important to keep salespeople motivated and moving forward in their performance. Managing around these two ratios will help managers avoid personality conflicts. Salespeople should regularly set goals to increase their closing rate and average sale. Upselling is one of the easiest and fastest ways a company can increase profits without spending an extra dime on advertising.

Strategy 8
Implementation Checklist

☐ Try to calculate your company's current average sale.

☐ Develop packages or offers to be added at the point of sale.

☐ Try upselling a week or ten days after the initial sale as well as at the point of sale.

☐ Test different offers.

☐ Evaluate the effect on average sales.

Telemarketing

Overview

Telemarketing is one of the most rapidly growing areas in direct marketing and one of the great opportunities for businesses to increase their sales and profits. Telemarketing is growing faster than direct mail, which continues to grow at great speed. Two-thirds of telemarketing is business to business; about one-third is business to consumer. Therefore, if your product targets other businesses, this strategy can become a very profitable marketing tool.

Telemarketing falls into three primary categories: follow-up, invitation, and sales.

The easiest way to begin telemarketing is by following up on a mailing. Telemarketing for follow-up involves calling your top customers and asking them if they received the offer. You can then remind them of the details and invite them to come and take advantage of the offer.

For example, if your company wholesales manufactured products to retail outlets, you could follow up a customer mailing with an offer like, "Good afternoon, this is Tom Smith with XYZ Company. How are you today? I was following up on our company's mailing to you about our new product lines. Did you receive the mailing? I wanted to let you know that we are extending this offer to our preferred customers through the end of this month and wanted to invite you to take advantage of it. Do you have any questions about the offer that I can help you with? Great. I hope we can serve you soon. Thank you and have a great day." There's no selling pitch here—it's simply a follow-up to a mail piece. This can increase the response of your mailing from 6 to 25 percent.

The second type of telemarketing extends an invitation. Again, this is not selling; it simply invites existing customers and perhaps new prospects to come in and take advantage of an offer. These invitations can be made not only to in-house lists but also to complementary customer bases. If you work with an upscale furniture store, for example, you could contact new home owners, making them a specific offer on your furniture and inviting them into the store to take a look.

The third purpose of telemarketing is to make a sale. One reason two-thirds of telemarketing occurs business to business is because businesses are accustomed to higher ticket purchases made over the phone. An average industrial order may be between eight hundred and a thousand dollars while an average consumer order might be in the fifty-dollar range. So telemarketing profitability can be dramatic for the business-to-business firm.

In this area of telemarketing, you can experiment with two types of approaches. One is a simple get-acquainted and lead-generation script, which inquires about customers' interests. It is followed up with a sales representative call or a piece of literature. The other approach involves using a memorized script. That is, you write down the benefits of your products and at the end of the script ask for the order.

If the order is a large-ticket item, you may want to generate leads for more experienced sale reps to follow up on. If it's a small-ticket item to consumers (under a hundred dollars), it can be sold over the phone and put on MasterCard, VISA, or American Express.

Be sure the script asks questions and follows up with features and benefits. You'll need to test different lengths of the script because it can be anywhere from a minute to five minutes long.

Remember that just as face-to-face selling closes about 30 percent of prospects, the same can happen over the phone. One rule in telemarketing as with any selling is to not waste your time with people who are not prospects. After a few questions in the initial part of the script, you can find out if you're dealing with someone interested in your product. If the person is not, say "thank you" and hang up. More stress in telemarketing is caused by people who try to make prospects out of people who aren't in the market for a particular product or service. This is a waste of time, energy, and money. Simply call, determine the interest level, and then move forward or get off the phone.

Implementation

Telemarketing is a form of direct marketing applicable in almost any type of business and any industry. It can be very inexpensive and makes the phone one of the most valuable marketing assets a company has.

Step One: Apply telemarketing to your company. Consider all the sales processes identified in Strategy 2. Ask yourself in what ways the phone can be used to strengthen or add to your sales processes—to follow up on mailings, to reactivate past customers, to encourage current ones to buy again, to follow up on prospects, or to make a sale (including as the first step in a two-step sales process; i.e., first generate a lead or prospect and then follow up with a sales letter or salesperson).

Step Two: Construct a script. Most telemarketing scripts will be short, first asking a few questions to determine whether the prospect warrants more attention and selling effort. You should introduce yourself and your company, and include your USP. Your script needs to be long enough to do what you want it to accomplish and no longer. Scripting should emphasize benefits that can be realized if the prospect or customer acts on your offer. Again, an important rule is to test. Try different scripts. You might want to hire or outsource some of the telemarketing efforts to companies that specialize in it. Depending on what you want to accomplish, the scripting may be oriented toward teleprospecting rather than marketing a product or service—that is, using the phone for locating and qualifying prospects for a presentation by a salesperson.

Step Three: Evaluate. A very important part of successful telemarketing is constant evaluation, testing, and tracking results. Make certain your callers keep good records of the number of dials made, contacts made with a decision maker, and resulting appointments or sales. Just like the other sales processes your company has, telemarketing has a closing rate. Make sure you know what this rate is and work to improve it with your callers.

Telemarketing for your company can be as complicated and sophisticated or as simple as you want. Phone systems are on the market that include telemarketing software for automatic dialing, headphones, and computer tracking of names and results. Or, you might see dramatic results just having a part-time caller come in for a few hours. Annual sales for one catering company grew from $300,000 to over $500,000 in one year when the company added a part-time telemarketer to set appointments for an outside salesperson.

Strategy 9
Implementation Checklist

- ☐ Choose which uses for telemarketing apply to your company:
  - Follow-up
  - Invitation
  - Lead generation
  - Sale
- ☐ Develop scripting, including the USP.
- ☐ Test, evaluate, and test again.

Marketing On-Hold

Overview

When you call a business these days, there's a very good chance you'll be put on hold, either briefly or for several minutes. Some companies play taped music while you wait or connect you to a radio station to listen to talk and commercials. Why not information about the company instead?

Phone on-hold marketing can be a powerful tool, automatically connecting callers to a soundtrack that plays messages of interest from your company. Special offers can be made and the features and benefits of working with your company explained. It's a great tool for exposing the consumer to your unique selling proposition.

There are probably companies in your area that specialize in this type of marketing. Ask for a free brochure and learn how the technology works. These professionals can select the music, create a script, and create a finished soundtrack, perhaps for less than you would expect. If you have the imagination and know-how, you can do your own piece, both music and voice.

To test on-hold marketing in your company, have specific offers with direct response and urgency elements just like a radio commercial. Invite the person to come to the place of business and take advantage of an offer by a specific time. Test different offers, perhaps having them coincide with some in the newspaper or on the radio. On-hold marketing offers a great opportunity for a firm to increase its exposure with very little increased overhead.

Implementation

Step One: Contact an advertising company or phone company with a division that specializes in "phone on-hold" marketing.

Step Two: Develop different scripts and test them. Make certain the scripting includes your USP and is built around benefits of working with your company, not the features of your product or services. Also, test making the phone on-hold marketing a direct marketing tool rather than just image advertising. Test offers that encourage people to respond. Ask them to come into your business and purchase or inquire about a special offer. This helps you better measure the effect of the technique.

Step Three: Follow up. Make certain that those answering the phone are capturing the names and addresses of those they talk to. This again helps leverage and optimize the phone on-hold marketing effort. If prospects have had a chance to learn more about your company while on hold, it is even more likely a follow-up effort will be effective.

Strategy 10
Implementation Checklist

- ☐ Select a company to work with.
- ☐ Develop messages, offers, and so on.
- ☐ Install messages on the phone system.
- ☐ Test.
- ☐ Capture and follow up.
- ☐ Evaluate, then test again.

Licensing Ideas and Strategies

Overview

When companies talk about assets, they generally refer to the accounting balance sheet that tells them how much cash is on hand and how much is invested in inventory and retained earnings. But every company also has valuable "hidden assets," those that are not on a balance sheet and many times are overlooked—successful direct mail approaches, powerful graphics used effectively in advertising, or salespeople with a particularly high closing rate. Perhaps the company has developed certain product lines that are unique or packages of products that generate more sales per customer than competitors. Perhaps employees are trained better than any one else's, or the owner holds a unique distinction in the industry. All of these ideas are assets that can be leveraged to produce extra revenue.

Once identified, some of these assets might be *licensed* to related companies outside your geographic area. If you're not planning to expand beyond your local operations, why not sell some of your successful ideas to out-of-town firms in the same industry? If your company has a proprietary idea that has increased your revenues, would it work in similar businesses? How much could you charge for these ideas? If your company licensed proprietary ideas to other firms, it could receive 10 to 15 percent of the increased profit. That is, if your idea produced an extra five hundred dollars and you received one hundred and five dollars, licensing this concept to twenty other companies would bring you an extra two thousand dollars a month. A person who licenses your idea has nothing to lose and everything to gain because it's risk-free and he or she pays only if it works.

You could license media advertisements or sales presentations and techniques that have been particularly effective, as well as upselling techniques and packaging concepts that have added to existing sales. If your business is a manufacturing or assembly firm, perhaps you've done well in keeping expenses down or in cutting operating costs. These ideas can be licensed.

If your company has a particularly talented salesperson, it may be lucrative to "license" that person's expertise to other firms. The flip side of this idea can also work. Watch for models in your industry that could benefit your operation and contact those that are outside of your area. Offer to pay them a licensing fee (percent of increased profits) for teaching you how to do certain things. You can then take these ideas and implement them in your own firm, increasing your sales and profits.

Implementation

The reason for the growth in franchising is that more and more businesses have developed successful systems in operations, marketing, and production that can be duplicated in other areas. The resulting "royalties" received can be impressive. However, there are drawbacks to franchising. It is expensive to launch, and it requires successful systems in all facets of the business. Not so with licensing.

Step One: Identify possible license opportunities. This is an advanced marketing strategy, requiring you to think in a new way. Most business owners or managers are so narrow in their thinking that they feel they have to hold onto every successful idea or their business will decline. In licensing, you step out of the three conventional ways to grow your business and simply leverage your assets in a different way.

Look at your business and company operation. Is there any facet in which you've developed a real expertise or advantage? For example, do you have a telemarketing script that works really well? Do you have a way to cut production costs that may be unique to the industry? Do you have an advertisement that routinely brings in successful prospects? Do you have a top salesperson who has created a winning presentation and enjoys a very high closing rate? Do you have a certain expertise in the industry that can be helpful to others in the same or even other industries? If so, list them for yourself.

Step Two: Document performance. After listing possible license opportunities, take time to document the performance of these ideas. In other words, just like a prospective franchise buyer would want to know of other successful franchises, prospective license buyers will want to know and be able to verify the performance of ideas in your business. Think of this step as putting together an offer for franchising your business. You'll want to be able to illustrate how the ideas can increase the revenues and/or profits of the prospective license holder.

Step Three: Make the deal. Identify the target groups of businesses and industries that could benefit from your ideas. Don't be narrow in thinking that a successful idea in the restaurant business wouldn't work in the clothing business. Be open and flexible in making your deal. If you can charge a fee for the license rights, great. However, you also might be able to arrange a commission or percent of the increase the ideas generate. The problem here is accounting properly. If you are able to implement the idea for the license holder and track the results, a commission or percent might work. You'll want to talk to your attorney in drafting a license agreement.

Step Four: Track the results. If your ideas are being used by others successfully, expand the selling of licenses!

Strategy 11
Implementation Checklist

☐ Identify highly successful methods for sales or cost cutting used in your company.

☐ Document performance.

☐ Determine businesses in your industry but in different locales that could benefit from these ideas.

☐ Make an offer.

☐ Test and evaluate.

☐ Identify models in your industry.

☐ Solicit their help; perhaps propose licensing their ideas.

Developing Seminars

Overview

A very effective marketing tool is the informational seminar. Employees of certain expertise in your firm present information and free advice to potential clients and customers. You can invite current customers to bring friends to the seminar, or you can market to certain demographic groups that would fit your company's customer profile.

You can offer such a seminar, for example, to clubs in the area who meet often and want speakers. If your topic is of interest, it will start gathering momentum. You can capture the names and addresses of all those in attendance and follow up on them later. Alternatively, you can send out a mailing piece to a selected demographic group. Capture interest by talking about the benefits of the seminar. Explain where the seminar will be held, and briefly describe the credentials of the person making the presentation. Often, if the person representing your company in the seminar is doing so for free, local newspapers and radio stations will run public service announcements. Ask those interested to call in to reserve tickets, and have the company receptionist capture their names, addresses, and phone numbers. (Though you can also get this information at the door, doing so beforehand tells you the size of your group.)

The first part of the seminar can be general information that addresses the topic you advertised. (Remember to tell everything—the more information you have and give, the more you'll sell.) After a break, you can come back and offer specific help and advice to those who are interested. Try to avoid selling anything outright. *Give* valuable information away. Always try to think in terms of your audience—what their needs are and how your service can benefit them.

If your product lends itself to a demonstration, this can also be an effective way to draw crowds at a seminar. You might be able to demonstrate a new technique of manufacturing, a particular item, or effective new marketing techniques. People yearn to learn how to do things in ways that are better, faster, cheaper, smarter, shorter, and so on. Consider creatively what resources are available within your company that are exciting or interesting enough to develop into an hour-long seminar.

If your company has particular low-end items you need to market, you might also look at showcasing these in a similar format, perhaps distributing them at the end of the seminar. It's a way you can give away free items or clear out inventory that needs to move. Always have on hand newsletters, brochures, and any other information vehicles that tell about your company. Follow up on those attending—get feedback and learn more about their needs and wants. You can then duplicate the demographics of this group with other direct mail or telemarketing efforts.

You can easily see how a seminar a month attended by fifty to a hundred people can add dramatically to your customer mailing list. If you don't have the company resources to embark on seminars independently, consider joint ventures with complementary companies who are successfully conducting them. Together, you can work out a share of the proceeds. This can get you into the seminar circuit without a heavy up-front investment.

Implementation

Step One: Determine the purpose of the seminar. Is it to attract new prospects? To improve the understanding of prospects so that salespeople can be more effective in closing? Or is it to get current and past customers to buy more?

Step Two: Determine the medium. Once the purpose of the seminar is determined, you'll need to decide which medium will be best in getting the purpose accomplished. If your product or service is for everyone, then perhaps an evening or weekend seminar in a meeting room at a suburban library would draw well. If your product or service is targeted to a specific group, then check with the program chairman of a lively club or professional organization. Or perhaps targeted magazines or newsletters would let you submit an occasional informational column of interest to their readers. This would help position your company as a source of expertise.

Step Three: Get an endorsement. If you can, try to get the seminar sponsored and endorsed by a third party. Even the sponsorship of a nonprofit or community organization such as the chamber of commerce can be effective. This lends credibility to the seminar and improves response because consumers trust in these third-party groups. It can also help cut the expense, as these groups often have continuous mailings or telemarketing to their members that you can tap into in promoting your seminar. Identify organizations whose members are buyers you want, and seek the group's endorsement.

Step Four: Develop a promotion piece. Again, this will depend on the target group you are promoting to and if you can get the seminar endorsed. Try to test your marketing first without a four-color brochure (which can be quite expensive). For instance, you might try a long sales letter that teaches and motivates prospects to come. This costs much less. Emphasize in the promotion piece how much education and benefit prospects will receive, even if they don't buy anything or end up working with your company. If you're charging for enrollment, make the offer risk-free through a guarantee that if they aren't happy, they can have their money back plus keep the workbook or other materials they received for attending.

Step Five: Follow up. If you use the seminar to teach and educate, it becomes very critical that you follow up with those who attend. Offer to provide free consultation or free information. Make an evaluation of their situation a natural extension of the seminar. Assume all those in attendance will sign up for the evaluation. Make it a standard result of attendance. With good follow-up, even a seminar that loses a little money or is free to attendees can be a very profitable undertaking. This is because your company has followed the strategies discussed in this book to create effective back-end selling opportunities that create revenue and profit.

Step Six: Leverage the seminar. Record the seminar. Adapt it to an audiocassette tape or newsletter. Use these transcriptions as handouts in your other marketing efforts. This will increase the conversion rate in all your selling processes.

Strategy 12
Implementation Checklist

☐ Determine which target group the seminar is for:

- Current customers

- Prospects

☐ Determine the medium.

☐ Try to have the seminar endorsed by a third party (i.e., customer or community group).

☐ Present the seminar for the purpose of "educating."

☐ Capture the names of attendees and follow up on them.

☐ Leverage the seminar in other marketing efforts.

Developing a Newsletter

Overview

With the increased availability of user-friendly desktop computer systems and software programs, it's faster and easier as well as less expensive to publish your own newsletter today. The idea is to educate, teach, and inform your prospects while also providing a vehicle for special offers or other marketing strategies.

A newsletter can be as short as two pages or as long as six to eight. You can mail it monthly, but at least four to six times a year to be effective.

A newsletter provides an excellent way to stay in touch, prove your expertise, lend credibility, and share special and beneficial information with your customers. Newsletters keep a conversation going with your clientele in between purchases. A newsletter can also introduce you to prospective customers, to test new markets, and to see how prospects respond.

The terrific advantages of newsletters are that they can be very flexible, inexpensive, and establish you or your company as an authority. They can be published right from your company and can grow into a profit center of their own. You might have several people write the newsletter so that there's variety of styles to keep each issue lively and readable. The paragraphs should be short, with short sentences and short words. Topics should be timely and relevant to your industry as well as to your business. Make good use of your computer's graphic capabilities.

Implementation

Step One: Determine which area of industry strength your company has and build the newsletter around it. The objective in this step is to set up your company or one of the company's owners or managers as an expert in your industry. This is very effective marketing. It can also be a USP in and of itself as you set yourself apart from your competitors. The newsletter's tools are as effective as the marketing principle they uphold: "The more you teach, the more you'll reach."

Step Two: Determine the distribution of your newsletter. Examine again your sales processes and integrate the newsletter into each phase. For example, teleprospectors can offer them as lead generators and previews before salespeople call. You can use them to announce workshops or other special seminars. They can be distributed by mail or as handouts at the counter. Test different channels of distribution, including direct mail and outside salespeople.

Step Three: Test. Test your distribution channels as well as your copy. Perhaps even try adding advertising to help pay for the publication cost. You'll also need to test frequency—let your prospects and customers tell you from their response how much is too much.

Strategy 13
Implementation Checklist

☐ Determine your focus.

☐ Determine your readership and distribution:

- Education

- Prospect follow-up

- Current customers

- Community

☐ Develop a schedule for printing, topics, offers, and so on.

☐ Test, evaluate, and test again.

Selling Unconverted Leads

Overview

After you have followed up on certain leads, you may determine your company cannot best service those prospects. Instead of letting these people go unserviced or uncontacted, there may be a source of revenue for your company in selling the leads to other companies.

One company developed an entire business selling leads to other companies. This was a travel company that gave away trips but on the entry form asked if people were in the market for an automobile, computer, financial services, and other products. The company then took this information and sold it to automobile leasing and sales firms, financial services firms, and so forth. The prospect that does not take advantage of your offer may be best served by a competitor.

The first step is to take the time to list all the businesses that would like access to your customers. These other companies may pay you to gain access to proven qualified prospects for certain kinds of products or services. You often can sell or rent your prospect list for a percentage of the resulting sales. You could also add other companies' products to yours.

For example, after a period of capturing names and addresses, you could have 4,000 recorded customers and another 10,000 prospects, all of whom might be perfect prospects for another business selling a complementary line of products. You offer these names to the other businesses, perhaps for a commission or a set fee. For this marketing strategy to work, don't be afraid to cooperate with a direct competitor!

You need to use your imagination and be creative. Make certain your company is capturing every name, address, and phone number of people who inquire or do business with your firm. (You will be doing what nine out of ten businesses don't do.) Over time, you will have a customer base that can be very, very valuable in bringing you ongoing sources of extra income.

Implementation

Selling unconverted leads is similar to working prospective customers; a lead, however, is a more qualified prospect. A lead is a prospect your salespeople may have contacted several times or your company may have sent mailings to several times with no response. A qualified lead is more valuable to another company than just a prospect.

Step One: Decide when a lead has been worked long enough. If several closing efforts have been made and still the prospect is uninterested, there may be a real objection that you can't overcome. Track leads so the company can determine at some point the lead is no longer qualified.

Step Two: Identify companies complementary to yours, even competitors. Joining together makes it more possible to close a qualified lead. These consumers are in the market, have contacted your company, and for some reason couldn't get serviced. So, join up with a competitor and share this information.

Step Three: Work out a compensation plan for the leads. It could be a simple fixed fee or it could be a commission. Either way is a gain for your company. The lead was going to be discarded, so why not try to leverage or optimize it (marketing asset) and turn it into a revenue source? Perhaps you can exchange your leads for those of another company. You can even offer to do a mailing to each other's leads.

Step Four: Test.

Strategy 14
Implementation Checklist

- [ ] Determine which prospects don't fit your company's target niche.

- [ ] Identify other companies in your industry that might better serve these prospects.

- [ ] Contact these companies.

- [ ] Work out a compensation plan (i.e., rental fee, sale, percentage, and so on).

Developing Community Involvement

Overview

Your company's community efforts become opportunities to market at a low cost. By utilizing opportunities to make an impact on the community, your company and its managers, employees, and owners over time become a community presence. When you're a noticeable part of the community, you increase your opportunities for commercial visibility and success.

You can connect with your community by offering special discounts or value cards to members of businesses located near yours, but schools in your community also represent excellent opportunities. Perhaps you could hold a demonstration at one or more schools or contribute goods or services for a school fund-raising event. You have multiple options for a "good fit"—day care, grammar schools, middle schools, high schools, private schools, religious schools, colleges, trades schools, or even a nearby university.

Look for opportunities with local charities and help them with goods and products to raise funds. One restaurant lets local charities sell $10 meal tickets to area residents. The charity keeps the entire $10, but the restaurant gets new customers. The restaurant has been able to break even or make a little money on the average meal because drinks (the most profitable item) are extra. More importantly though, the individual customer or family comes in from the charity sale and the restaurant keeps track of them, inviting them back for more business. The possibilities are limited only by your imagination.

Charitable involvement, though laudable and effective, is not the only community opportunity, however. A transmission repair facility owner was a member of the local Automobile Service Association, which held regular group meetings. He said that beyond what he had tried in direct mail and other advertising aspects, his facility's number one source of business came from his involvement in that group, in getting referrals from other store owners. Make certain you, your owners, and your managers participate in local groups and associations. Chambers of commerce often form organized groups that get together for breakfast or lunch each week. Cards are handed out and leads are exchanged on a regular basis. This is the type of activity your company needs to be involved in all the time. If possible, join several of these organizations and have company representatives regularly attend meetings.

Following are some other ideas:

- Establish relationships with community stores. Offer to distribute their brochures if they'll distribute yours. Put up their signs if they'll put up yours. Include their circular in your next mailing if they will include yours in theirs.

- Post signs or circulars on local bulletin boards— supermarkets, general stores, churches, clubs, and so forth.

- Donate your product or service to community agencies and institutions.

- Get your company name in local print and broadcast media as much as possible. Keep your name and the benefits of your service foremost on the minds of local residents.

- Make special offers with mailings to clubs in your community: health clubs, social clubs, service clubs, recreational clubs, and so on.

- Advertise on billboards, buses, parking meters, and other highly trafficked, visible areas.

Implementation

Community marketing offers a way for a small or medium-sized business to compete for image with the large businesses. Large businesses are more likely to have a budget for image marketing (i.e., advertising and marketing focused on getting your company name and a positive image out to consumers). It's different from direct marketing, which seeks a direct response and is accountable and measurable.

Step One: Identify groups and associations you or your company would like to join. Such a list can be secured from your local chamber of commerce. The objective of this step is not to find groups you want to have lunch with each month, but rather to find those with business members who can lead your company to more prospects. Your company should join groups that actively promote networking and alliances.

Step Two: Form marketing alliances with these groups for the purpose of accessing their customer base. In return, allow them to market to your customer base. Form alliances with companies you can endorse. Your goal in this step is to use your community groups for exposure to more prospects.

Step Three: Attend the meetings regularly. Hand out business cards. Offer to give workshops or luncheon presentations. Contribute to the newsletter. Build your image while capturing prospects' names for follow-up marketing. Become visible in the community without spending an extra dime on advertising.

Strategy 15
Implementation Checklist

☐ Obtain a list of local groups and associations.

☐ Identify which groups or associations can best help your company find more prospects.

☐ Attend meetings regularly and get names of members.

☐ Prospect these members, seek referrals, and cross-promote.

Getting Free Publicity

Overview

The key to free publicity is contacts. Take stock of who in your company knows writers and editors of business publications, or those that deal with your field (science, cars, computers, real estate, home services, etc.). Learn who knows the owners of newspapers, radio stations, and magazines. The closer the contact, the more coverage you'll get.

Take time to send out press releases illustrating how your company or product solves the problems the editor talks about in his or her column. It's one thing to simply send out a press release with a black-and-white photo and hope; it's quite another to send it, call up, and say, "Hi, Joe, let's have lunch tomorrow. I want to tell you the story about the public relations material I sent you earlier this week."

You can join press clubs in your area as well as other groups media professionals belong to. Business owners should learn which restaurants media people frequent and invite them to lunch in exchange for discussing a press release.

After the publicity appears, milk it for all it's worth. Follow up every press release published and use it as a mailer to contact former customers and current customers. Use it as an insert with other circulars.

The key to free publicity is to have newsworthy information that solves consumers' problems. An auto repair facility that provides a twenty-point checkup to used car dealers on their used cars is sitting on a marketing strategy. To pitch the local paper or radio a story about a twenty-point checkup probably wouldn't get any takers. But if the repair facility slanted the story to emphasize that they're working to decrease the amount of used car frustration that local buyers feel, that becomes a news item.

Address your release to a specific department—sports, entertainment, or business, for example. Get the name of the editor in that department. Put the date in the upper left-hand corner, followed by the name of the person to contact for more information. Include your phone number. Indicate the release date ("For Immediate Release," "For Release Week of May 15," etc.). Next, provide a headline. Double-space your descriptive copy. If you need a second page, identify your story at the top of that page in the upper left corner. And to indicate the end of your release, type the pound (#) sign or an asterisk (*) centered below the last line.

What should you say in your release? State who it is about, what it is about, where it is taking place, when it is taking place, why it is taking place, and how it came about. Write in short, clear sentences that offer facts, not opinions. Accompany your release with a short note (handwritten, if your prefer) and explain in a few words why you're sending the release. And, where appropriate, enclose a photo. Send the release about ten days or so in advance of the date you wish the information to appear.

In an effort to make your press releases as newsy as possible, you can tie them in with the news of the day. For example, during a very cold winter, the news release might be that your battery store agrees to charge batteries free for one day. You could stage an event or a free seminar in which people could learn how to use your product or service. This would work well for a computer facility. You could give away an award or a scholarship each year. Use your imagination and do something incredible.

Understand that free publicity may not result in immediate cash or new marketing dollars for the company. What you will find, however, is that these efforts enhance every other marketing effort. You'll find that the other marketing tactics provided in this book will take hold much more quickly in your community when people see your name and recognize your community presence. Plus, it saves advertising dollars.

Implementation

Step One: Find your "hook." Determine whether you have something newsworthy or important enough to the general community to "sell" to a local editor for free publicity. You want to do the same as any paid public relations firm would do—find a reason the press should talk about your company without charge! It may be your USP. It might be a unique patent or product feature that improves your industry. It may be that your industry is growing rapidly and that the growth trends are important for the community to know about. If you or your company is positioned as the expert in the industry, you can offer trend projections that would interest the community.

Step Two: Create the news release. There are several types of news releases:

- *Executive appointments,* which announce the appointment of someone to a new position

- *Community involvement,* which publicize sponsoring events or get-togethers

- *Industry forecasts,* which predict trends or performance

- *Topical news,* which relate to trends

An example of an executive appointment news release appears on the next page.

Step Three: Keep selling. In seeking free publicity, your customer is the editor. Just as a customer whom you want to buy your product needs several closes before they say "yes," an editor may need to hear from you often before publishing your press release. Don't give up. Be persistent. Remember, this is *free!*

FOR RELEASE: January 14,1998

CONTACT: Bob Brown   -or-   Tom Jones
               XYZ Company   XYZ Company
               (000) 555-1234   (000) 555-5678

XYZ COMPANY EXPANDS LAS VEGAS STAFF

LAS VEGAS—XYZ Company, a manufacturing firm that recently expanded operations in Las Vegas with the acquisition of ABC Company, has appointed three new employees to its staff.

Bill Anderson, a former account executive in XYZ's Oregon office, has been named regional sales manager for the company's Nevada operations. In this position, Anderson will oversee all marketing and sales efforts for offices in Reno and Las Vegas. Prior to joining XYZ, Anderson spent more than twelve years in international sales and marketing training for another manufacturing firm.

Randy Blake and Susan Smith have accepted newly created account executive positions for XYZ and will be responsible for representing the company's services to Las Vegas–area business owners.

A recent transplant to Nevada, Blake spent twenty-seven years helping California aerospace and high-tech companies with strategic planning and corporate development.

Smith, who also moved to Las Vegas from California, worked for nearly ten years as an investment broker.

Step Four: Capture inquiries and follow-up. Make certain you leverage your press release by including an offer or announcement of a workshop in the release. This is to optimize the release for marketing gain. Keep track of prospects that respond to the release. Follow up and make your sales presentation.

Strategy 16
Implementation Checklist

- ☐ Determine which product or services may be "newsworthy."

- ☐ Develop contacts among local editors and media representatives.

- ☐ Craft your press release.

- ☐ Capture respondents' name, phone number, and so forth.

- ☐ Follow up by phone, mail, or a combination.

Making It "Easy" to Buy

Overview

This one suggestion could increase sales in your company 15 to 50 percent. So many businesses make it difficult for the customer to buy, such as by closing on Saturday or maintaining operating hours that don't reflect customer needs.

Hours of operation are an important convenience. If yours inhibit consumers or other businesses from taking advantage of your service, then work to change them. Further, you may want to offer some of your most valuable customers special times for shopping or doing business. Perhaps stay open one evening just for them. Look at what the competition does and improve on it.

Make sure all major credit cards are accepted, such as VISA, MasterCard, and American Express. You might even consider in-house financing or credit accounts. Allow customers to purchase by fax, phone, and mail as well as in person, if that's feasible. Time is a precious commodity.

Help prospective customers learn about your business easily. List your business address and phone numbers wherever prospects could be looking—brochures, newsletters, receipts, invoices, and so forth. Have toll-free lines available to help long-distance customers access your company more easily. You may want to look at putting your company's products in a catalog and mailing it to your current customers, making it easier for them to shop. Offer them information, products, and other services they can benefit from.

Give away as many samples as possible. Offer guarantees of "no risk" to the consumer. Many businesses do not have confidence in their product or services. Their guarantee includes stipulations in fine print that really cancel all guarantees. Customers should be able to return the product without hesitation for a refund or exchange it for another product. Your guarantee should remove all risk from the customer.

Many times companies will charge small prices for services that, if given free, would have a much higher perceived value and increase both the number of sales and the size of the average sale. For example, one store was charging two or three dollars for alterations in clothing. By providing this free, people bought more quickly than before.

Implementation

Step One: Consider all policies. In this step, take a fresh look at all your company policies and procedures. This not only includes sales and marketing but production, administration, customer service, management, purchasing, and so forth. Talk to customers and find out in what areas of your company they suggest changes. Listen to your staff and employees too. Listen to what salespeople give as reasons that sales don't close. All of these efforts will begin to uncover policies and procedures that inhibit customers from spending money with you. Very importantly during this step, remain open-minded—don't hang on to traditions or policies just because your company has had them for twenty years.

Step Two: Remove policies and procedures that stand in the way of customers buying. As you research to find what policies and procedures might be making it "hard" to buy, change those that can be quickly altered. These might include hours of operation, financing, or production techniques. Perhaps your customers want easier packaging of products and services. Understandably, you can't remove policies right away that might have a serious impact for your company. Look at each policy and procedure as a profit center. Does having the policy increase revenue more than the cost of implementing it?

Step Three: Test. You don't have to keep policy and procedures written in stone. If you try to change and it doesn't work (or hurts profitability), then you can always return to the old way. Again, the importance of testing is evident. Evaluating whether a change was successful or not will most likely depend on profitability. However, you may decide to do something unrelated to profit—that's the right of an owner. As long as you keep "making it easy to buy" as an objective, you will see the company increase in revenues and profit.

Strategy 17
Implementation Checklist

☐ Review all policies and procedures that involve customer interaction.

☐ Remove any policies that inhibit customers from doing business with your company.

☐ Test results.

☐ Regularly review policies and procedures from a "marketing" viewpoint.

Constructing a Yellow Pages Ad

Overview

Your business may or may not need yellow page advertising. If you do use this outlet, the following strategies can help you get more return on your advertising dollar. Plus, these same strategies can apply to Internet and Web Page advertising.

Your yellow pages ad should have a headline that catches people's interest and identifies a major benefit or unique selling proposition. Using short paragraphs and bold headings, you can catch people's interest and tell them what they need to know about your products and services. (Remember that the more you inform and teach, the more sales your company will make.) Make certain the ad has a call to action. At the end of it, tell the customer exactly what he or she should do—whether it be to call and make an appointment, get a free quote, or learn more about the service. Emphasize your guarantees, and make certain you identify any distinguishing characteristics that set you apart from competitors.

What does your company want the ad to accomplish? Most small to medium-sized businesses cannot have an ad taking up space that does not generate sales. A direct response format allows you to measure results from a yellow pages ad (i.e., directing people to call and ask for a specific service). One way you can measure response is to have the phone number in the ad ring a dedicated line.

Implementation

Step One: Construct a yellow pages ad concept around your USP.
Check out the ads of your competitors. Your objective in this step is to highlight your USP with a headline or slogan that will clearly differentiate you from them. When people need something now, they scan the yellow pages. They'll be more attracted to your ad if a clear USP is evident, such as "Eyeglasses ready in an hour."

Step Two: Write your ad copy. Make certain that you include the following elements in your ad:

- Headline (USP)

- Direct response copy (ask the prospect to do something, such as call, come in, etc.)

You might also consider one or more of the following:

- Offer (include a compelling offer to come to your business)

- Free appointment or free information booklet

- Special for first-time customers

- Preferred Customer Club with special benefits

Step Three: Try different ads in different directories. Or perhaps show a couple of different versions to customers and prospective customers, asking them to tell you which is more compelling. Make copies of the ad to use in prospecting and in mailings.

You need to use good judgment in designing your ad. Remember, the objective of yellow pages salespeople is usually to sell you more space or color, which does not always mean more business. Again, remember the valuation of the success of your ad, if it is profitable. Judge profitability by the lifetime value calculation of one customer, not the initial first purchase.

Strategy 18
Implementation Checklist

☐ Consider what you want to accomplish with a yellow pages ad.

☐ See that key elements are in the ad:

- Headline

- Direct response copy

- Offer

- Instruction to customer

☐ Test the ad, perhaps in different directories.

☐ Evaluate the results.

Employing Unused Inventory/Specialty Items

Overview

If you were to check the storage facilities of companies around the country, you would find years of inventory sitting on shelves. Many companies fail to realize that this is one of their greatest marketing assets.

Unused inventory items can be turned into bonuses or gifts on a package offer. For example, a store might give away a pair of socks if the customer purchases a shirt and pant outfit. These socks may have been in inventory for months. You also can send items through the mail to current customers or as enticements to attract new customers. See that the inventory is used if it's not sold.

After you have exhausted the inventory possibilities, look to specialty items as marketing tools in and of themselves. Look in the yellow pages under "advertising specialties," and you can access a host of catalogs with thousands of items available. Many of these items will cost only a few dollars but have very high perceived value to the customer. There are also catalogs that offer free items in combination with purchased items. Use the gifts to get people into your place of business or to seek more information from a letter or phone call, or even to make a purchase. People love gifts. The number one word used in marketing is "free." There's never been an exception to this rule.

Some traditional ad specialties are calendars, T-shirts, ballpoint pens, and scratch pads. Use them to put your name, address, logo, and so forth in front of prospects every day. As special incentives, you can try electronic gizmos such as desk clocks, micro calculators, and the like. Companies involved in sponsoring teams have T-shirts, baseball caps, buckles, lighters, plate frames, tote bags, key chains, and numerous other items imprinted with the company name and logo.

Gifts will generate leads, goodwill, and enhanced credibility in the community. They will also generate increased profits. Look to utilize all product assets available and develop them into specialty items that can be distributed in the ways described. Alternatively, if you ultimately have inventory left that is not only unused but also apparently useless, you may be able to sell it! Call a professional liquidator and he or she may find a buyer for your leftovers. Talk to a barter company and trade inventory for cash or other services.

Companies spend hundreds and sometimes thousands of dollars to give away specialty items like pens and refrigerator magnets. Instead of spending money on these items, why don't you go back and see if there are inventory items you can give away?

Implementation

Step One: Take an inventory of products available. See if your company has excess stock of items they currently sell, or even items from years past. There is value in these items—they can be regarded as a marketing asset.

Also check other companies and see if they have excess inventory or stock. Many times this stock is already written off as "sunk costs." See how you could use these items in marketing your company.

Step Two: Determine marketing uses for the product. Consider again all the sales processes you uncovered in Strategy 2. In these sales processes, the excess product or inventory can be used for lead generation, thank you gifts, bonuses or premiums for buying, and even trade or barter. In working this strategy, it's again very important that your company understand the lifetime value of your customer. If winning a customer means he or she stays with you for ten to fifteen years and spends hundreds or thousands of dollars, then giving away inventory that has been written off can be a very cost-effective marketing strategy. If your company is in need of services but short on cash, bartering can provide a way to preserve cash and use inventory.

Step Three: Contact a specialty company. It may be that you can have some printing put on your inventory to help promote it. Perhaps you can add value to the inventory by adding other items such as pencils, cups, T-shirts, mouse pads, and so forth. Specialty companies can help you promote your company without spending a lot of money. Sometimes promotional items can be more effective than advertising with media.

Step Four: Combine your inventory with specialty items and test them in your promotions. Try using these extras in the different sales processes to see if your ratios in closing and average sales can be increased. (This is another reason why it is very important to now have these two figures tracked and understood in your company.) This strategy is designed to increase both those ratios by using inventory, stock, and specialty items that cost very little.

Strategy 19
Implementation Checklist

- ☐ Take an inventory of products available.
- ☐ Develop uses for the product:
  - Lead generation
  - Thank you
  - Bonus or incentive
  - Trade
- ☐ Contact a specialty company, and consider bartering. Determine if what they have might boost your sales and profits.
- ☐ Test, evaluate, and test again.

Utilizing Brochures as Direct Response Pieces

Overview

Brochures have many advantages in that they can convey information and teach consumers about your business. People read brochures when they want information and data. They're interested in learning more about your company and having enough visuals, photos, illustrations, charts, and graphs to make a correct decision.

Another great advantage of the brochure is that you can use it as a follow-up to less expensive advertising. You can run smaller media ads asking prospects to send for a brochure. Invite them to call or write for free literature, and from there you can send out more advertising without spending more on print advertising, radio spots, or television ads.

If necessary, consider changing the size and/or pattern of folds of your current brochure so that it will fit into a business envelope. This will enable you to use the brochure in communicating with the current customer base as well as new customers. You don't need to use a lot of color. Use the space to convey information.

Very importantly, use your brochures as direct response pieces. If your a place of business sees a lot of traffic, many times salespeople can't get to every customer. However, if there's a brochure displayed prominently, customers can take it with them as a starting point in gathering information. Further, it should have a detachable reply card or a toll-free phone number to call on a specific offer in the brochure.

Another form of "brochure" that is growing in popularity is the videocassette. Look at your company's products and services to see if a ten- to fifteen-minute video would be an effective means of communicating your message. You could have this tape playing continuously at your place of business or it could be utilized in trade shows and booths. Many companies mail videocassettes to qualified prospects instead of mass mailings of brochures. It would be wise to follow up this type of mailing with a phone call. Have the cassette returned if the prospect is not interested.

Implementation

Step One: Analyze your company brochure. Ask yourself, "Does this brochure really help make sales or is it simply an image piece?" If your company has the budget for the latter, fine. But if not, you might want to consider making changes to the brochure to better leverage or optimize its expense. You might even be able to dramatically lower the cost. Read the copy carefully to make certain it is "direct response" oriented. Make sure it tells readers exactly what to do and how and when to do it, and asks them to take action on an offer. Also determine whether a video would be applicable and/or feasible.

Step Two: Make changes. In this step, you'll want to make changes to the brochure that better leverage its use. You want copy that "sells." Take the presentation of your best sales representative and see that much of it is in the brochure. Overcome objections. Ask for the order. Give the customer or prospect a reply mechanism such as a phone number or prospect to send back. Even consider changing from a color brochure to a long sales letter. Or, create a sales letter and have the brochure added to it for more sales impact. In this way, you can keep old brochures before changing and do the selling in a sales letter.

Step Three: Follow up. To further leverage your brochure investment, make certain your company has a follow-up system in place to improve the closing rate of prospects contacted with a brochure. Not only follow up on replies sent in, but test the profitability of following up with all those mailed.

Strategy 20
Implementation Checklist

☐ Analyze your current brochure.

☐ Make changes to enhance its marketing value:

- Copy needed to "sell"

- Offer

- Mailing size

- Reply mechanism

- Direct response

☐ Follow up on the brochures that are distributed.

Using What's Working

Overview

One of the major marketing mistakes companies make is they stop using marketing approaches that worked in the past. They don't calculate the profits from those marketing efforts, erroneously conclude the program was a failure, and never use the tactic again. For example, when retailers were asked what marketing medium they find most effective, 46 percent responded "direct mail." Yet if you go into these retail outlets, you'll find that many of them did a direct mail piece at one time, concluded it was ineffective, and discontinued mailings.

Visit with someone who's been around a while in the marketing area of your firm and ask what marketing tactics worked well in the past. You'll be surprised to find that many of these ideas have been discontinued. Either management changed or the person in charge failed to determine the marketing technique's profitability.

One company mailed an offer to their customers and sold two products from the effort, with net profits totaling a few thousand dollars. The owner concluded that the mailing was a failure due to only two responses, yet the several thousand dollars in revenue minus the cost of the mailing (two to three hundred dollars) constituted a profitable performance. Another firm placed a small ad in an automobile publication advertising a free checkup on used cars. When asked if the ad worked, the owner confirmed it had. When asked if it was still running, he said no. Realizing the error, he put the ad back in the paper and immediately saw results again.

You might also take time to look through the yellow pages of other cities. Call companies in similar industries and identify the successful ones. Ask them questions about the marketing ideas they have implemented and found successful. Can you imagine how simple this is? Yet, it can be fantastic in returns to your company. Find successful models in your industry and adopt their strategies.

Finally, go back to print ads you've used in the past, radio spots, and any marketing you've done through groups or associations.

Meet the best salespeople that have worked for your company and find out if their ideas are still being used. If not, reinstitute them. Consistency is a key to increased earnings. If you will take the model ideas that are working for companies in your industry and that have worked for your company in the past and keep them consistently implemented with a couple hours of effort a week, your company will realize increased sales and profits.

Implementation

Not only is this strategy a leverage of marketing assets—not doing it is a big marketing mistake!

Step One: Conduct research. In this step, you want to uncover all the successful marketing, advertising, and sales ideas your company has used in the past. Interview sales people and staff members who have been with the company a long time. Talk to the owner and managers who have been working with the company the longest. Go to old advertising files and look up former ads, letters, and other marketing materials. Determine which ones worked in the past but now are not being used.

Step Two: Implement old marketing strategies that were once profitable but because of employee turnover, or simple forgetfulness, are not currently being used. Reinstate these strategies. You will want to make certain the USP is integrated into all the strategies. Many of the ideas that didn't work before might now work with a good USP and follow-up systems in place.

Step Three: Find industry models. Take some time in this step to research and locate the companies that are models in your industry, both in your local region and outside it. Look closely at the marketing strategies the leading companies use. Without violating copyright or trade law, adapt some of these ideas to your own situation. If a company does not want to share its successful ideas with you, propose licensing the idea and offering compensation for it. If it can save your company years of practice and expense, it may very well be worth it.

Step Four: Test, evaluate, and test again.

Strategy 21
Implementation Checklist

☐ Identify past successful marketing strategies.

☐ Reinstate those that worked but were for some reason discontinued.

☐ Research model companies in your industry to identify and adopt successful ideas (licensing them first, if appropriate).

☐ Test, evaluate, and test again.

Offering Back-End Products

Overview

Once you have the names of all your customers and those inquiring about your firm recorded in a database or file, you can communicate with them on a regular basis and reward them by offering new opportunities to purchase your product. This is called "back-end" marketing, a very profitable strategy.

Chances are, however, that after your company made a one-time sale to those customers, it's left them alone. This may be because the company doesn't feel it has anything else to offer them. If you're in real estate sales, after you sell a new home to a customer, he or she becomes a logical prospect for furniture, landscaping, plumbing, additional contracting or repair work, and additional products that complement a new home. You should become a sales representative for those other services.

Let's say you work with a store that sells satellite systems for the home. After the initial sale of the satellite dish, you could come back a month later with offers for big-screen televisions, VCRs, and other entertainment products. You could follow up later with an upgraded system for the first customers who purchased an older satellite system.

Suppose your company manufactures swimming pools. After you make the initial swimming pool sale, there are a host of opportunities for back-end complementary products: patio furniture, barbecue grills, and deck accommodations to name a few. Or perhaps a Jacuzzi and hot tub. Make certain your company is providing the regular maintenance program for the pool.

There are three ways you can implement back-end marketing in your company. First, see what products your company can offer after the initial sale. If you are in the clothing business and certain types of clothes are purchased, be sure to come back regularly with other wardrobe options. If you work for an insurance business and it makes an initial sale in health insurance, make certain that all other insurance and financial products are offered regularly on the back-end.

The second area in which you can work back-end marketing is in complementary line products. As in the example of the real estate, satellite, and swimming pools, take a look at your own company and see which products your company does not carry but which complement the line of products your customer purchases. Offer these complementary products to your customers. The third way to profit from back-end marketing is to simply rent your list and work out a deal with a share of the sales or profits with the other firms' product lines.

Many companies do not understand the great value in working the back end. They should understand that customers who are satisfied are much more easily persuaded to buy again. Be sure to tell your customers exactly why you are inviting them to purchase and exactly why you are offering them that service.

Back-end marketing opens your eyes to the concept of a customer's lifetime value. Many companies feel that the one-time sale is the value of their customer. If they produce an effective back-end marketing offer on a regular basis and the customer buys two or three more times during the year, then the value of that customer times the number of years that customer is with the firm is increased dramatically. When your company understands the lifetime value of a customer, the budget for marketing becomes an investment rather than an expense.

Implementation

The concept of back-end marketing was introduced as part of the strategy of working with current customers. Refer to that section for more information. Simply put, back-end marketing means that after your company has made an initial first-time sale, it has a system in place to make regular contact with these customers and give them the opportunity to do business again. It is a deliberate effort to increase the value or worth of your customers.

Step One: Capture and record information. Learn what your customers buy, when they buy, and how much they buy.

Step Two: With this information, develop back-end offers tailored to the customer. The more targeted your offers can be, the better success you'll have. Make sure that all company products are cross-sold and related products are offered systematically. Then consider the relationships you have with other companies. See whether their products or services complement yours and can be offered to your customers.

Step Three: Build the value of your customer base by tracking how well back-end offers do and how often the mailings are successful. With this information, you can bring additional profit to the company by making the list available to other businesses. You can do this as selectively as you want, or you can give the list to a list broker who sells it across the country.

Step Four: Test, evaluate, and test again.

Strategy 22
Implementation Checklist

☐ Capture and store customer information.

☐ Determine the products and services available after an initial purchase:

- From your company

- From another company with complementary products

☐ Determine whether your list of customers could be made available to other companies through:

- Joint ventures

- List rental

- Percentage of sales

- Endorsed mailing

☐ Test, evaluate, and test again.

Arranging Consignments

Overview

If your company is crowded for office space but has product that sells, consider consigning the product to another outlet. One company was involved in three sporting equipment product lines—soccer, cross-country skiing, and golf. This owner had a very small retail establishment in a strip mall area. Customers loved the product and they loved the owner and his service. He was a referee and coach for local youth teams.

With his contacts around the city, this businessman took some of the material he couldn't stock and secured space at other sporting outlets complimentary to his product line by working out a deal with the owners for a percentage of the sales. You can do this for retail establishments and for wholesalers. Suppose your company manufactures a water-saving device that sells for two hundred dollars. You could consign two of these to fifty different plumbers in the area. They could market the device after a plumbing service call to a home or business. If they called on twenty customers each (one thousand total customers a week) and 2 percent purchased the device, that would be twenty sales at two hundred dollars or four thousand dollars. If you gave the plumber one hundred dollars, that would be extra income for him and a few thousand dollars extra a week for your company.

Another company manufactured toner cartridges for laser printers. Rather than hire and train an entire sales force, the company made a presentation to one of the large paper distributors in the area that had twenty-five to thirty salespeople. These salespeople called on hundreds of customers a week to resupply them with paper products. The manufacturer consigned the laser cartridge at wholesale to the paper distributor and thereby increased the company's exposure in the marketplace considerably.

Implementation

Step One: Determine if consignment fits your situation. Does your product need exposure to a lot of people? Is your location limited in providing this exposure? If the answer to these questions is "yes," then consignment may be an effective marketing strategy. Identify your products that require greater exposure.

Step Two: Identify consignment locations. Look first within your own geographic selling area and try to identify companies that service customers who are similar demographically to yours. These business owners are the ones you should approach.

Step Three: Establish the arrangement. You can give the business owner a percentage of sales from your product, fee for space rental, or even an offer to consign that company's product at your location. Or, if your location is poor, you can work out a mailing to your customer base.

Step Four: Test. It's important here to identify a pitfall to successful consignment. Most of the time, your product will not get sufficient attention or sales promotion to sell well. Part of your arrangement thus needs to include a clear understanding of how much selling and promoting the other business will give your product. Offer to provide sales training or promotional material. Do all you can to see that your product is given attention at these locations.

Strategy 23
Implementation Checklist

- ☐ Identify products that could sell well in other locations.
- ☐ Approach business owners of these locations to take your product on consignment.
- ☐ Set up the arrangement:
  - Percent of sale
  - Renting or leasing of space
  - Cross-promotion
- ☐ Test, evaluate, and test again.

Offering a Catalog

Overview

In this age of micromarketing, you do not need a customer base of a hundred thousand to produce a profitable catalog. Time is becoming such a precious commodity to consumers that even a small company or a narrow line might benefit from catalog offerings.

A catalog does not have to be full color, glitzy, and fancy to be a great marketing tool. A nice three- or four-page black-and-white version with substance and information will accomplish a lot.

You can send your catalog on a regular basis to your existing customer base (consider installing a toll-free order line). Plus a catalog is a great way to acquire new customers. You could send out a few hundred to a list of likely prospects and see what response you get.

Again, the key is that the more you tell, the more you sell. The catalog allows your company to tell its story and get its name out while making it easy for people to "shop," thus helping your loyal customers stay loyal more conveniently. You can learn a great deal about your customers by keeping track of what they purchase out of the catalog and what they like and don't like. This will help you know what to keep in inventory.

With desktop publishing, the catalog does not need to be expensive. Be specific and direct in outlining the benefits of your product. Use drawings and photographs and test to see which one works best. Look at some of the best catalogs and adapt their order form to yours. Always mail during your industry's peak selling time, but test other times of the year as well.

Implementation

Step One: Determine the prospects for your product selling in a catalog. The key variable in this determination is price and markup. A catalog is, in a sense, your sales staff. You need a good markup to profitably sell in a catalog; therefore, you might also want to contact national catalog companies to see if they will carry your product. They definitely will want a high markup. For example, if your product costs five dollars to produce, a catalog company will want to sell it for twenty dollars. And different catalogs will cater to different buyers, so prices will vary.

Step Two: Consider other products. By adding complementary lines to your catalog, you may be able to pay for the cost of producing it. You might want to try your own products at first and expand from there.

Step Three: Create and produce the catalog. Don't start with a big investment in a four-color piece. Start with a few pages of black and white. You may need to add some color or eye-catching graphics if your product requires some emotional appeal. You can create simple catalogs on an in-house computer or outsource the task to a graphic designer, if you prefer.

Step Four: Leverage the catalog's use. In this step, consider all the sales processes in your company and add the catalog where you can along each. Use it for prospects, past customers, and current customers; to present your primary line; and to market all your back-end products or services.

Step Five: Test, evaluate, and test again.

Strategy 24
Implementation Checklist

☐ Determine whether your company has a product line that might sell in a catalog.

- Lead generator

- Back-end marketing

☐ To expand your catalog, approach the owners of complementary product lines.

☐ Create the catalog; test black-and-white before full color.

☐ Determine the use of the catalog:

- For prospects, past customers, and current customers

- To present your primary line

- To market your back-end products or services

☐ Test, evaluate, and test again.

Implementing the "Both Barrels" Approach

Overview

Ultimately and ideally, your company will benefit most from a comprehensive marketing plant that covers all your bases. Picture yourself as a four-star general planning a strategic assault on the marketplace, and you'll see you need every bit of fire power you can muster.

1. **Letterhead, order forms, and invoices.** See that all of your company forms have your logo and unique selling proposition spelled out as briefly and clearly as possible. You can turn the invoice into a follow-up form by asking sales clerks to note future recommendations on it for the customer. Include on work orders both what was done and what's recommended to be done. (This can be put into a database and followed up on). These forms should say "thank you" and make it easy to purchase again.

2. **Inserts and postcards.** Newspapers are trying to target prospective customers by publishing certain issues for specific ZIP codes. They'll usually allow you to include an insert and access thousands of prospects affordably. Inserts work best if you make a specific offer. You might combine coupons with inserts. Test different ZIP codes and offers, and stay with the winner.

3. **Inside sales signs.** Inside signs help establishments advertise current sales and specials. Include your USP on any signs you print. The signs can offer packages for sale rather than individual items. Salespeople can be trained to turn to these packages and, using upselling techniques, increase the size of the sale.

4. **Circulars.** You can employ part-time students to distribute thousands of circulars a week. They can be used as door hangers and placed on windshields of cars in parking lots. Have workers target areas where people are frequenting businesses likely to have the same customers that your business appeals to. Circulars cost very little and enable you to target your audience better than a mass media campaign.

5. Classified ads. Many products can be sold over the phone with classified ads. Test different classified ads in the publications you select for your product or service. Many publications that are distributed to every home offer very reasonable classified ad rates. Direct readers to call for additional information. If they call, have a recording explain the product and direct them on how to order. This ties in with inbound telemarketing and can be a very low-cost, effective way to increase profits for your business. During phone sales, don't forget to offer back-end products. You'll want to test different prices and different ads. If the headline and copy are well written and the recording tells enough about the product and how to order, classified ads can be an effective tool.

6. Reprints of ads and publicity. If you're able to pursue many of the ideas talked about in this book, you may be writing some ads and articles. Leverage these ads by reprinting them or blowing them up to poster size and putting them around the store. Send them out to customers and prospects, and get as much from those reprinted ads and publicity articles as possible.

7. Gift certificates. Gift certificates can be an ongoing offer from your company. In your marketing, remind people to ask about them. You can have them produced in specified dollar increments if your prefer.

8. Testimonials. Many companies have been in business for years and have never recorded a testimonial. Gather them from your satisfied customers and use them in your marketing.

9. **Special local events.** Have your company represented at all local events, especially those that attract customers like yours. Consider sponsoring and co-sponsoring events with other companies. Have a booth or an information center where you can capture names of prospects. Always be where the traffic is. Appropriate special events for you may be seminars, workshops, presentations, parties, contests, community activities, fairs, and/or carnivals.

10. **Consultations.** Take an inventory of the knowledge assets on tap in your firm. It may be that one of the salespeople, owners, or managers could offer consultations for a fee. They could do this by phone, through the mail, or in person, providing expert advice for complementary industries.

Implementation

As you consider this group of ten ideas, you'll see that they're vehicles for making sure you integrate your USP into all your marketing efforts and into all your points of contact with prospects and customers.

Step One: Determine a group of marketing ideas you can easily implement.

Step Two: Implement each idea, making certain the USP is in each one.

Step Three: Test, evaluate, and test again.

Strategy 25
Implementation Checklist

☐ Identify a group of ten ideas to test.

☐ Implement each idea.

☐ Test, evaluate, and test again.

Conclusion

The twenty-five strategies showcased in this
book can play a big part in helping your
company grow in sales and profits.
Remember, the unique approach each of these
strategies involves better leveraging and optimization of your company's *current* marketing
assets for more profit.

These ideas do not require additional spending on advertising, they don't take a lot of time to implement, and they can be continuously worked, tracked, and modified. Your employees don't have to be marketing experts to implement or manage them.

Very importantly, as you apply these strategies, you will begin to think about marketing differently. You will automatically turn first to your existing assets before spending money in the acquisition of more. As you operate with this new mind-set, your company will enjoy ongoing growth in sales and profits for years to come.

Successful Direct Marketing Techniques

Getting People to Buy Your Products and Services

Nothing happens until you get people to buy your goods and services. You can have a great product and the perfect market, but what if no one will buy? Your sales message must communicate a reason and enough benefits to persuade a buyer to buy.

As a business owner, you can use direct mail in working with your customer base or expanding your business with new products and services.

In either case, direct mail is salesmanship in print. The best way to illustrate how to market your product by mail is to examine the steps a professional salesperson would complete while selling you a product in your home:

- The salesperson will first capture your interest, and then build on it to get you to stay with him or her during the presentation. He or she will have to see that enough excitement is generated in the very beginning, or you will tune out and say "no" at the end of the presentation.

- Next comes a presentation full of benefits and features. The salesperson will illustrate exactly how the product will benefit you and make your life better. He or she will tie the features of the product to its benefits.

- After describing the features and benefits, the salesperson will always offer a bonus or guarantee, followed by an incentive for you to purchase that day.

- Finally, a good salesperson will simply ask for your order.

This process is also the essence of mail order and direct mail. *Mail order* may take place without you sending any sales literature about your product. People will simply respond to an ad for your product, which in turn you will send through the mail after receiving their payment.

Direct mail, on the other hand, implies that you are sending literature that tells enough about your product to ask for the order, or just enough to compel them to lift the phone and order or inquire further. You then follow up with additional brochures and information in which you ask for the order.

Direct mail involves direct response. That is, you communicate something to a prospect and ask for a response—to phone in an order, to send in a coupon, or to request more information. The purpose of direct response with your mail order program is to generate a reply, either positive or negative. If consumers send in the coupon along with their money, or come into your store to buy, you've made a sale. If they don't, you'll never get a rejection, but you won't generate any revenue either.

As the particulars of direct mail are discussed in the next several pages, keep in mind the concept of salesmanship in print. You want your mailing piece or ad to do the same thing a successful salesperson does when selling you a product.

Elements of Effective Direct Mail

Certain elements are common to all successful direct mail, whether you're inviting previous customers to buy again or seeking new customers. As you work with each of these elements and test different ones against each other, you will perfect your direct mail efforts and get the results you need for your business to thrive.

These elements, which we will discuss in detail, are as follows:

- Uniqueness/positioning
- The opening or headline
- The presentation or copy
- The offer
- The call to action/urgency/close/bonus
- The guarantee
- The postscript

Uniqueness/Positioning

Whether you're selling a product through the mail one at a time or working to increase volume sales, you must find your singular niche in the marketplace. You must identify your *unique selling proposition* (USP) before using direct mail. Do this by closely examining the competition and determining what void is not filled—then fill it. If you have a manufactured product that you sell through the mail, determine what features and benefits you can assign this product that are unique. Position your product in the minds of your prospective customer through price, quality, service, or perhaps a guarantee that is unique among all your competitors. It should appeal only to qualified prospects.

After you choose an area in which to distinguish your product, get specific. For example, if your price is lower than the competition's, then state that you offer the lowest price (or that you'll offer a better price than the best they've found). Or if your product's quality is superior, then specify why or how it's different: How much longer will it last? How much better is the material? How much better is the workmanship? How much money will customers save because they use your product instead of a lesser-quality one? Assign specific numbers to these attributes. Will they save two dollars? Will it last one year longer? Is the material 40 percent better? Is your service available twenty-four hours rather than daytime only? It's very important that you determine this unique selling proposition in order to position your product in the mind of your consumer (perhaps you can provide some free samples and have consumers describe to you what they sense is unique about it).

Lacking a unique identifier, the only variable the consumer will consider is price. And unless you're absolutely lower than everyone else in your market niche, your product will have little chance of selling.

Headline or Opening

Knowing your unique selling proposition helps you produce "grabber" headlines for your print pieces. It's the ad for the ad. It says *you*. From the unique selling proposition comes the few words or succinct idea that gets the attention of the prospective buyer and encourages him or her to learn more about your product.

As you read various newspapers, peruse magazines, and flip through direct mail offers, you will notice that the ads and letters you stop to read are those that grab you early, right up front. The headline illustrates a direct benefit to you, the customer. This feature or benefit is so powerful that you're encouraged to read more.

If you're going to invest in any type of marketing to sell your product through the mail, you must come up with headlines that instantly convey your unique selling proposition or some aspect of it. The basic function of a headline is to take the reader's eyes from the opening down into the copy of your ad or sales letter. Following are some headline examples:

- Get Rid of Money Worries for Good

- Two Men Who Wanted to Be Independent in the Next 10 Years

- Any Four for Only $1.00

- How to Get Rid of an Inferiority Complex

- No Time for College—Take College Home

- Order Christmas Gifts Now . . . Pay After January 1st

- Free to High School Teachers—$6.00 to Others

- How I Improved My Memory in One Evening

- How $20 Spent May Save You $2,000

- How a Man of 40 Can Retire in 15 years

- They Laughed When I Sat Down at the Piano, But Then I Started to Play!

- Do You Make These Mistakes in English?

- How a Strange Accident Saved Me From Baldness

- Are You Ashamed of Smells in Your Home?

- Car Owners . . . Save One Gallon of Gas in Every Ten

- Double Your Money Back If This Isn't the Best Soup You've Ever Tasted

- Greatest Bible News in 341 years

- How I Became Popular Overnight

- How to Feel Fit at Any Age

- How You Can Get a Loan of $500

- Seven Ways to Break the Overweight Habit

- To a Man Who's 35 and Dissatisfied

- To a $15,000 Woman Who Would Like to Be Making $30,000

- You Don't Have to Be Rich to Retire on a Guaranteed Income for Life

- Can You Spot These Seven Common Decorating Sins?

- Thousands Now Play Who Never Thought They Could

- I Lost That Ugly Bulge in Two Minutes

- How to Make Money Writing Short Paragraphs

Such headlines come from the unique selling proposition. They provide the attention grabber that summarizes a distinct benefit for the buyer. The same effective headline can be used in classified ads, display ads, and direct mail letters, as well as in radio and television spots. Regardless of the method you choose to get your product sold, headlines serve as one of the most important elements of successful marketing.

You'll notice in many of the headlines reproduced above that certain words show up over and over. The top words (in order) to use in our headlines are the following:

You

Your

How

New

Who

Money

Now

People

Want

Why

Here are some others that also prove effective:

Exciting

Remarkable

Improvement

Announcing

Bargain

Challenge

Certain basic consumer needs have motivated purchases for years and are not likely to change drastically in the future. These needs, which you can develop headlines around, are as follows:

Health

Appearance

Getting ahead

Making money

Careers

Saving money

Bargains

Winning friends

Winning praise

Gaining status

Leadership

Happy marriage

Children

Improved education

Low stress

Low embarrassment

Low discomfort

Low boredom

Leisure

Security

Saving time

Saving energy

A headline can be utilized in all the methods of direct marketing: classified ads, display ads, magazine ads, newspaper ads, radio, television, postcard inserts, inserts in papers, coded mailing lists, ad specialties, card packs, yellow page ads, newsletter reports, telemarketing scripts, and brochures.

Remember that headlines not only appear in the text of an ad or at the top of a letter—they can serve as teasers on the outside of envelopes. No one will read your sales letter until he or she first opens the envelope. And in some instances, 97 percent of recipients will throw away the envelope. Even your own customers.

As you determine the priority for all of the elements identified at the beginning of this chapter, headlines should receive 70 to 80 percent priority. In constructing a headline, it's important first to determine the uniqueness of your product. For example, if your product's uniqueness is *quality,* try words such as the following in the headline:

Good

Better

Exclusive

Improved

Special

Unsurpassed

If the uniqueness is *information* or *news,* you can use the following:

    Announcing

    Today

    New

    Now

    Suddenly

    Recent

If the uniqueness of your product is a *specialty item* or a *surprising aspect,* you can use the following words:

    Astonishing

    Amazing

    Fantastic

    Striking

    Surprising

If it is *price* or has to do with money, try these words:

    Fortune

    Bargain

    Reduced

    Lowest

    Discount

If the uniqueness is in your product's *appearance* or *use,* these next words can prove effective:

Attractive

Elegant

Dramatic

Classic

Exquisite

Colorful

If your unique selling proposition lies in *saving people time,* you can use such words as the following:

Helpful

Usable

Reversible

Powerful

Workable

Handy

Certain phrases also have proven very successful in headlines:

Gift

Free Lesson

Free Trial Membership

Free Use for Ten Days

Free Literature

Free Booklet

Free Estimate

Free Demonstration

How to Make Money

How to Avoid Depression

How to Conquer Low Self-Esteem

How to Improve Your Reading

How to Enjoy Life

Your headline needs to be specific—the more so, the better.

If you run a mail order business where you simply place an ad in a newspaper or magazine, the headline is all important. Prospective buyers read through hundreds of classified ads looking for what they want, and only those with eye-stopping headlines will catch their attention. Your successful classified ad will stand out as unique.

However, if you fail to get adequate response, it may be that prospects do not have enough information to make a decision. Perhaps you need to supply more detail to entice more people to order. In this case it can be helpful to use a two-step approach. Create a headline in a classified ad that directs the prospect to follow up for a free report or more information.

If your product is a higher-ticket item, it likely requires more promotion and explanation than a simple classified ad can provide. You may be more successful with a sales letter of two or three pages that does the same thing that someone would present face to face, or maybe one that tells just enough to encourage the reader to order more information.

Go through some national publications and look at headlines. Pick up one of the tabloids and see firsthand why they sell so well—the headlines are terrific! They grab you at the checkout stand and entice you to read more. Keep a shoe box full of headlines. Gather them based on what attracts your attention. Listen for good headlines on radio ads and jot them down. Try to analyze why they're powerful.

In summary, the headline needs to be short and easy to read, instantly understandable and simple in its message, and as specific as possible. It is the most important element of your marketing effort because it gets your message noticed.

Presentation or Copy

Advertising or marketing really starts to become an art in the text of the mail piece. After a headline has successfully attracted readers' attention, the copy must keep them interested and take them all the way through the sales process.

Recall again the salesperson in your home selling you life insurance or other products. The top professionals are the ones who can keep your interest for the hour. If a salesperson is not specific in illustrating features and benefits and then asking you questions, it's likely you will tune out and wait for the presentation to end so you can decline the offer.

This is the challenge with your mailing piece. Whether it's a classified ad, an invitation to buy again, or a seven-page sales letter, the copy must accomplish your objective. If the product is inexpensive and uncomplicated, then perhaps a simple ad with a few sentences of copy and benefit description will do. The bottom line is that copy must be as short or as long as necessary to accomplish the purpose of your ad or sales letter.

Marketing copy should be written as if you were talking to the prospective buyer face-to-face. Avoid getting technical and wordy. Describe the features in short, concise paragraphs, and illustrate the benefits along the way. When you sense there may be a question about a particular feature or benefit, ask the question in your copy, then answer it. This can be very effective.

The copy segment of a marketing piece exists to create interest and desire. The copy must showcase the most powerful claims and benefits of your product to keep reader interest building. It's the "stage setter" for your offer and close. It creates the bonding process and qualifying method by which you work with the prospect through the procedure of ordering your product. Very importantly, it's the explanation of your headline. For example, if your headline reads "Ten Ways to Feel Like a 20-Year-Old Even If You're 60!," you could move on in the copy as follows: *Yes, it's true, we have discovered it—the secret of youth. And it can be yours whether you're 50, 60, or 80 . . .* In the next several paragraphs you would describe how the formula was discovered, what scientists worked on it, and so forth. The goal is to keep creating interest in and building desire for your product.

The copy should list all the benefits of the product. It should build a compelling case and prove the rewards. It should bring testimonials and endorsements and perhaps the results of independent testing or analysis of the product. It should describe unique features and benefits—price, selection, convenience, attractiveness, experience, or whatever is appropriate to highlight.

An effective method to writing copy is to make it appear editorial in nature. Construct it to look like a news story. Following a compelling headline, your paragraphs should be short and perhaps preceded by a sub-headline. Many times effective sub-headlines will be the questions that the reader or listener may have.

Unless you believe in what you're writing, the reader probably won't either. Try to convey this belief in simple words, as if you were talking face to face. Make the copy conversational and easy to read. Use short, vivid, colorful words. Talk to readers as you would in person, creating a spoken rhythm to your copy. Asking questions can be more effective than making statements. Be sure to describe more benefits than features of your product. Number the benefits and place them in order. Consider putting your letterhead at the bottom of the page to leave room for headlines at the top. Summarize your offer in the headline and repeat it several times throughout the copy.

If you're going to use testimonials or referral names, place these at the beginning to establish credibility, and then refer to them again throughout the copy. Case histories supporting your claims can also prove effective. Illustrations of product use will increase the response to your offer, so give as much of this information as possible. Remember, *the more you teach, the more you'll reach*. Describe how specific use of your product will solve problems or enhance the reader's status in life.

If your product carriers a higher price, justify it in the copy of your ad or sales letter. In the same vein, spell out any savings as clearly and as quantifiably as possible. The word "free" is still one of the most powerful stimulators in good copy. Use it when appropriate from start to finish. In addition, frequently weave in the twelve most persuasive words in the English language:

Save

Money

You

New

Health

Results

Easy

Safety

Love

Discovery

Proven

Guarantee

After you've completed a draft, put the copy aside for a time and read it again to see how you can improve it. Get rid of unnecessary words and strive to keep the copy flowing in short, readable paragraphs. However, don't conclude that a short letter is the only way to garner sales. Long letters frequently pay off, and long copy can be very effective in display advertising. Many times traditional advertisers will encourage a lot of white space, but a headline and effective copy can pull ten times the return of a white space ad. Just remember the AIDA formula:

A Attention with headline

I Interest

D Desire

A Action

Effective copy, or the presentation portion or your ad or sales letter, is enhanced with the human factor. If you include testimonials, avoid sensational comments and instead use real-life experiences. Ask a satisfied customer to illustrate how your products solved his or her problem, and perhaps include a photo. This approach sounds like the truth because it is the truth. Consumers are very skeptical of advertising, and anything that is exaggerated will turn them off instantly. Sincerity is the name of the game.

Your Offer and Call to Action

The offer you want to propose to a customer can be illustrated in your headline. You could extend a two-for-one offer or a specific price break. The offer should be restated several times through the copy of the ad or the copy of the sales letter. The important thing is to accompany the offer with a call to action, where you tell the reader or listener exactly what to do:

Order Today!

Respond by . . .

Send for Your Free . . .

Call Immediately!

The call to action is the same as a salesperson asking for the order. You might synopsize the benefits and descriptions of what the customer is getting and then ask for the order. Do, however, add an element of urgency to your call to action: "Hurry!" "Last Chance Offer" "Limited Quantity" "To Those Who Qualify."

Several marketing devices can stimulate responses and help consumers take action, such as phone numbers, coupons, or order cards. Other effective incentives can be an information request form, a special report request, a preapplication, or an ad specialty such as a calendar or ruler. You also can improve response to your offer by giving a bonus. Let consumers know the bonus is available for a limited time, and that if they act today, they can qualify for it. Each of these devices is geared toward making certain that prospective buyers clearly understand you want them to respond and how to do it.

Guarantee

A guarantee creates a very effective closing tool that makes an offer even more appealing. The guarantee should place the entire risk upon you, the seller, rather than any on the buyer. It could be a lifetime guarantee or for the life of the product. You can offer a specific time guarantee, a 100 percent money-back guarantee, a replacement guarantee, or a specific performance guarantee. You could offer to replace the product or give 100 percent value on trade-in.

Many companies offer an examination period that gives customers a few days or a couple of weeks to decide whether to purchase the product. You could offer a month or even a whole year money-back guarantee. This is called *risk transfer*. The seller takes the entire risk instead of leaving it to the customer. Give the buyer two or three times the customary review period to make the purchase nonthreatening and nonintimidating. Throw in bonuses worth more than the cash price of the product. Let customers know they can even keep the bonus if they ask for their money back. Many companies who have adopted this better-than-risk-free guarantee have found that it's a profit center in and of itself. That is, more revenue is generated because of the guarantee than lost because of returns.

Postscript

After presenting the offer, bonus, and guarantee, close the sale. A call to action is made, and the pitch is completed. Well, not quite. An effective addition to the sales letter or even to the display ad is a postscript. This device gives you an opportunity to restate your offer, terms, bonus, guarantee, and primary benefit in just a single paragraph. It also reminds consumers how to order the product. This can be very effective because after opening a sales letter or when reading an ad, people tend to look over the beginning and then go right to the end. Thus they'll take in your headline and your postscript. In the postscript, they'll find everything summarized for them, which will either encourage them to order right away or go back and read more for details.

The postscript could go something like the following:

Only the first 100 respondents will be able to take advantage of this offer to eliminate baldness, and for only $49.95! Never before have you seen hair grow so quickly. You'll be loved and admired by your friends and neighbors. Be sure to order by December 23, in time for Christmas. Your satisfaction is 100% guaranteed, no questions asked. Don't hesitate. Order today by calling 1-800-555-1234, or send in the easy sign-up enrollment card below with your check, money order, or credit card. All credit cards accepted. Order today!

This summarizes the entire sales letter or copy of the ad, an effective tool in improving the response to your mailing.

Putting Together Your Direct Mail Package

Each direct mail effort you launch consists of a "package."

If you're producing and/or selling an uncomplicated, lower-ticket item, then you may need only to place an ad in the classified section of a targeted publication, ask for payment, and when money comes in, send the product to the customer. If, however, you offer a higher-end item and the product is more complicated, or you need to present the sale in a two-step approach, then you'll have different parts to your package: the envelope, the sales letter, the brochure, the response device, and the reply card/envelope. The postage class/rate you select also has a bearing on your overall success.

The Envelope

In direct mail marketing, the whole objective of using an envelope is to get your letter opened. Properly used as a copy carrier, the envelope can generate excitement and pique the recipient's interest in seeing what's inside.

Narrow the headline from your sales letter down to a few words and run it in the lower left corner on the front of the envelope. This is referred to as a "teaser." (There may be some restrictions with the post office in what you can place in that area of the envelope, so check with your local authorities.) Analyze on a daily basis the envelopes that *you* open. You may notice yourself responding to teasers that say something like "Free information inside" or "Your guide to $50,000 a week" or "Limited offer—please respond within 10 days." The important thing is to condense the most powerful, image-making words of your message to evoke the curiosity you need to have the letter opened.

Make the mailing look like a personal letter—use plain white and, where possible, have the address typed. Avoid labels, and create the appearance of the letter being first-class mail. The outside of the envelope might say "Personal." You can also put something distinctive in the upper left corner, such as "Office of the President," "Executive Director," or "Treasurer."

If your letter is opened, your teasers and plain white envelopes have worked. The important thing is to test which approach yields the most profitable response. Keep records of the envelope devices you use and how they perform.

The Sales Letter

Once you have determined the form of envelope you want to use, the next important element is the sales letter within. Details of an effective sales letter were covered in the previous chapter, but again remember that you'll want to make the copy as long as you need to make a sale. If you operate strictly with mail order, and your product line is fairly simple and low ticket, the sales letter may not be necessary.

The key is to make certain to cover all the objections and completely describe the benefits. Your "conversation" with the reader should convey a warm, friendly approach. Start the sales letter with a headline and follow it with all the reasons for purchasing. Answer any hidden questions, and persuade the reader to *act*.

The Brochure

Though the sales letter should be a one-on-one conversation piece, the brochure can be technical. Here you can talk about the product in more detail, with a lot of facts and descriptions of benefits. This piece also can contain excerpts of your best testimonials or endorsements. Start it with a headline or titling on the order of "Special Offer," "Reasons for Ordering," or "Product Summary." Then be as specific as possible, covering all the data that backs up your sales letter. You can also use space in the brochure to restate the points of the sales letter and ask for the order.

The Response Device

The response device is the part of the sales letter and/or brochure that closes the deal. It gets your customer or prospect to act. If the headline has been effective and the body copy is filled with benefits that are appealing, at this point you need simply to tell recipients how to act. Tell them to get on the phone and call the reserved line to order the product. Tell them where to get a coupon to bring to the store. Tell them to complete the enclosed request form and mail it today. Invite them to come back to the store, or to call and add the purchase to their charge account. Enhance the closing by offering a guarantee that is easily understandable and totally risk-free. In every case, be very specific. Any time the reader is unclear on how to get your product and start benefiting from it, he or she most likely will not respond.

The Reply Card/Envelope

The advantage of including a coupon or postage-paid reply card is in tracking your response rate. On the coupon or card, simply summarize the offer and the appeal: "Yes, I agree with your offer, and I am accepting your 100% guarantee plus the offer to keep all the bonuses. I will take you up on the guarantee for the next three months. If it doesn't perform as promised, I will send it back and expect a full refund. On that basis, here is my order."

If the reply piece is not a self-mailer, include a postage-paid reply envelope. Make it as easy as possible to respond. Eliminate any potential reason for hesitation.

Postage Rates/Class

You have several options in mailing to your customers and prospects, each appropriate to certain contexts and applications.

First class vs. third class. Generally speaking, a first-class, "personal-looking" envelope will pull the best response. However, the decision of whether this is your best route will depend on the size of testing you want to accomplish and the size of the eventual roll-out campaign. You might test on a first-class basis, and then roll out to a third-class postage.

The advantages of first class are faster delivery, forwarding to new addresses, handling with dignity, improved response rate, and improved delivery. Some of the disadvantages are that it's the most expensive option and there may be some weight constraints.

Third class has the advantages of lower initial cost and a greater weight allowance.

Some of the disadvantages include slower delivery, no forwarding, anywhere from 15 to 30 percent lost, and less respect in handling.

Bulk mailing. After you run initial tests in smaller quantities, you can mail in quantities of two hundred or more pieces at lower prices. Permits run anywhere from fifty dollars to seventy-five dollars for a twelve-month period. Bulk mailing simply indicates that the pieces are bundled by ZIP codes. In bundles of ten or more in the same ZIP code, bulk mailing pieces can go out (at the time of this writing) for thirteen to fifteen cents each. Contact your local postal authorities for current rates and bundling guidelines.

Take a look at the final package you put together and ask yourself, "If this were to arrive in my mailbox today, would I open it?"

Telemarketing

Telemarketing is one of the fastest-growing forms of direct marketing today. It provides an opportunity to make one-to-one contact with prospective buyers at a very low cost. Telemarketing can be used to expand your current customer base, improve the dollar amount per sale, improve the company's customer service image, and create an opportunity for follow-up sales. It can be used to generate leads for outside salespeople, to sell a product directly over the phone, or to provide an incoming service for consumers who request additional information. Products ranging from twenty-five-cent fasteners to ten-million-dollar airplanes can be sold over the phone, as witnessed by the following examples:

- One national company's telemarketing operation did $35.2 billion in over forty-five different telemarketing centers with two-thousand employees selling a range of products from $1.98 medical accessories to high-tech energy systems.

- Another office began analyzing its customer base of two thousand. The analysis showed that 68 percent of these customers generated just 6 percent of sales. This told the regional manager that he couldn't make any money on accounts that spent less than three thousand dollars a year, so he turned them over to a team of telemarketers. In the first three months, telemarketers generated more than $12,000 in sales. An inactive account that was activated placed a $24,000 order with the telephone salesperson.

- A material distributor in Chicago used telemarketing to go through a twelve-thousand-name customer list, learning that key accounts made up about 2 percent of the list. Thirty percent of the customers were eliminated from the list because they had gone out of business or changed business. The remaining accounts were prioritized as A, B, or C accounts, based on annual purchases. When a program was thus developed to update the customer list, it resulted in sales.

Telemarketing not only is becoming a growing tool for small businesses, but for individual entrepreneurs as well. Further, telemarketing prices have been coming down while mailing prices have been going up. With the cost of hiring salespeople, training them, and getting them into the field, more companies will find the value in telemarketing. Following is an overview of the ways business owners can utilize telemarketing as an effective direct marketing tool:

- **Communicating with current customer base.** An effective use of telemarketing lies in following up with direct mail offers to current customers. Retail clerks and other sales staff can be assigned a certain number of customers for regular contact. This is a very inexpensive way to increase customer loyalty and to improve the response to any offer mailed to the current customer base. This is part of one-on-one marketing, a tool by which companies can secure loyalty on a long-term basis from customers.

- **Retail/wholesale promotion.** Whenever a new product is offered, or the store or company wants to promote a certain product, telemarketing can serve as a great testing tool. Telemarketers can call out to current customers as well as use lists from complementary businesses with similar customer bases to test the response. A telemarketing team can follow up on ads currently being placed or a separate promotion effort. They simply invite people to take advantage of the opportunity by coming down to the store or company within a certain time period to receive the product.

- **Appointment setting.** Telemarketing may be utilized as a way to save outside direct salespeople time and energy. Outside salespeople are very expensive to maintain, and to use them in less productive activities such as appointment setting can be costly. Individuals hired to work from the home as well as large-scale telemarketing operations can be engaged to set up appointments for salespeople, or for estimates, or dental checkups, or free consultations— whatever your area of interest.

- **Service.** Telemarketing can be a valuable way to communicate to a customer base the importance of service in your company. People love communication, and when they get a telephone call letting them know about a particular service, it builds loyalty toward your company or product.

- **Customer follow-up.** Once a prospect has become a customer, additional back-end follow-up opportunities should be made. Not only check on how the product is doing for your customers, but offer additional products maybe two or three weeks after the initial purchase. This will not only enhance the sale, but will let customers know that they're an important part of your company's business.

- **Surveys.** Marketing surveys can be a very useful tool in determining demand for a product line. Especially if the product is for business, telemarketers can make inquiry calls before too much expense is incurred in generating industrial clients. A survey questionnaire can determine the level of demand or interest in a proposed product.

- **Price testing.** Telemarketing provides an effective, very inexpensive way to determine whether the price set for your product is one that will work in a direct mail campaign. Call different segments of a list with different prices. Find out which price works best in each area of the country.

- **Direct mail follow-up.** A combination of telemarketing and direct mail creates a very powerful campaign. You can expect responses to increase ten times more than the mail program alone. This also offers a great way to test the list of your direct mail program. Many times you can rent a list starting with just a few hundred names. You can call and test to see whether they are the type of customers you want to use as the basis of a direct mail campaign.

- **Prospect qualifying.** Telemarketing can be effective in screening out prospects who would not be interested in your product. Only those who are qualified would be followed up on with a mail campaign or with a phone call from an outside salesperson. You can take time to qualify the prospect as to interest level, time period for purchases of products like yours, and income and age variables.

- **Pre-literature mailing.** After telemarketers have narrowed down a list, the remaining prospects can become targets of mailing literature, which increases contact and gives them more information. This can be followed by a phone call from a salesperson for an appointment or for closing the sale on the product. Again, it depends on the product price range and complexity.

- **Upselling.** Telemarketing can be a great tool in increasing the size of a sale. Once a customer makes an initial purchase, a phone call should follow that offers additional products before that customer's order is shipped. If one out of ten agree to additional products, you can see how a telemarketing campaign can greatly increase the sales amount.

- **Straight sales.** Is there a product available in your company that could be sold directly over the phone? This is especially effective when you have an established and loyal customer base. If your company doesn't have any, locate other similar companies and purchase appropriate products at wholesale rates. There are wholesaling sources throughout the country offering inexpensive products that allow for a 200 to 300 percent price markup. Make your selection(s) based on the type of product the customer has purchased in the past.

- **Follow-up to incoming inquiries.** If a prospect is told to call for more information, it's important that an experienced salesperson be on hand to turn that inquiry into a sale.

Telemarketing Scripts

In all telemarketing efforts or programs, a script must be provided for the telemarketers to use. There are several benefits to having a written script:

- **Consistency and accuracy.** Management needs to be certain that the same message is presented to customers or prospects each time. The script also helps the telemarketer to stay on track and not create any misrepresentation. By having a written script, telemarketers are more comfortable in what they say. They are not thrown by offhand remarks from customers. They are not tempted to drift into unknown, uncharted waters.

- **Accountability.** Various scripts can be used to test different offers and different telemarketers. As results are tallied, scripts are evaluated: Accounting determines the profitability of an offer or a telemarketing approach. The same written script available to different telemarketers can be a great indicator of weak performance.

- **Measurable daily activity.** By having a written script, management can begin to determine how many sales approaches should be made per day. Knowing exactly how long the script is helps in determining the number of calls and sales that should occur. It brings predictability into the equation. It helps in hiring and in setting sales goals. It also helps in getting telemarketers to the point quickly and politely, resulting in a shorter time per call and more calls per hour.

Scripts can be designated as *closed* or *open*. A closed script is one that allows only for a single response—a sale or not. An open script is one that accommodates handling one of several responses. This could be a response for an order, or more information, or a salesperson to call. These responses are tracked and passed on to the appropriate department or salesperson.

Rules that are very similar to those for a direct mail sales letter apply to writing a script. You should first establish a clear objective as to what the phone call is designed to accomplish. Then use very simple conversational language. Try not to be technical or evasive. Be as straightforward and as honest as possible. Don't attempt to confuse or mislead the prospect.

In preparing the script, overcome as many objections as possible. Anticipate answers to routine questions and objections before they are voiced over the phone. Construct questions that can be answered with "yes" or "no" rather than allowing the customer to ramble in his or her answer. Include a "thank you" phrase at the close of every telephone script. Keep your scripts as brief as possible, but not so brief that customers do not understand the nature of and reason for the call.

Following are some sample scripts for various telemarketing situations.

Incoming calls:

Customer: "I received a postcard in the mail today" or "I'm calling on the ad I saw in X publication. I'm interested in receiving my travel membership."

Operator: "Great, let me get some information from you." (He or she then records the name, address, and phone number of the buyer.) "On the front of your postcard [in the ad] is a number in the right-hand corner. May I have it please?

"All right, Mr. Jones. You've been selected to get our travel club membership at the preapproved discount of $49.95. Along with that is a catalog that's filled with all the travel benefits you'll receive from our club. This will save you a lot of time, energy, and money in traveling. Our travel club gives you high-quality products at prices well below retail. These prices are only available to our members.

"The membership is $49.95, but this also allows you to purchase other travel services from our 300-page catalog. I'll ship your package out today. Let me take your charge card information now."

Outgoing calls:

Telemarketer: "Good evening, Mr. Brown. This is Susan with ABC Travel Company. How are you today?"

Customer: "Fine."

Telemarketer: "I'd like to tell you about the new travel card promotion we are calling you about today. If you have a few minutes, I'll explain our program." (Pauses, then continues) "This month only we can send you our travel card at a low discount of $49.95. This allows you and your family discounts at hotels and car rentals and other attractions across the United States. You will save up to 50 percent on your next vacation. How does that sound, Mr. Brown?" (Pauses, then continues) "The cost of this membership is normally $100 for one year, but we are offering this special today for $49.95. This is a savings of over $50. Mr. Brown, I can reserve your travel card right now and mail it today. You'll also receive our catalog, which includes over three hundred additional money-saving travel opportunities. This package is valued at over $500 and is yours free with your order today. May we mail your travel card to your current address, Mr. Brown? Are you still at 145 Second Street?" (Pauses, then continues) "Thank you, Mr. Brown, for your order. You will receive your card by return mail."

Follow-up on a direct mail piece:

Telemarketer: "Hi, Mr. Brown. This is Susan with XYZ Company. We wanted to follow up on the mailing you just received describing our new promotion this month.

"I would like you to know that Mr. Jones, our president, has authorized me to make available to you an additional preferred customer discount. If you take advantage of our offer this week, we will subtract another 10 percent from the special indicated in the mailing. In view of this extra value for our preferred customers, could I take your order now and report to Mr. Jones your favorable response? Thank you for being a preferred customer with XYZ Company, Mr. Brown."

Record Keeping

Whether you conduct an in-house or outside telemarketing effort, records should be kept regularly. Telemarketing operators should keep track of the name, address, and phone number of each individual called. Further, the outcome of each call should be recorded as follows:

- No answer

- Not available

- Not interested

- Call back

- Send literature

- Order taken

- Do not contact again

A daily log or record sheet of every number dialed should be kept, and a master record of all individual logs should be made daily. The individual can keep an individual call report while the manager does a daily master record sheet. The individual report includes the data and response for each phone call, indicating whether more telemarketing follow-up is needed, whether an order should be filled, or whether a new customer has been added to the customer base. There can also be a section to capture other information when the customer or prospect indicates a special situation.

A master record sheet tallied from all the individual ones should indicate how many orders were made, the percentage of calls that resulted in orders, how many of each item was ordered, how much literature was requested, how many contacts were not interested, and the total number of completed calls (that is, prospects or customers reached). You can also record the total calls dialed, number of hours worked, and so forth.

Hours of Operations

It is generally recommended that most telemarketing shifts run from three to four hours. During a day, telemarketers can reach from fifty to one hundred customers; during a four-hour shift, twenty-five to fifty. Customers in the evening can number between sixty and one hundred during an eight-hour period or half that for a four-hour shift. Generally, if you have telemarketers operating from home, they function anywhere from two to three hours per shift.

Many new state laws limit the period of calling (e.g., not after 9:00 p.m. or before 7:30 a.m.). Commercial sales projects should avoid Monday mornings and Friday afternoons as well as near closing time.

Telemarketing can be a very powerful direct marketing tool. With the tremendous increase in specialty phone numbers (such as those with a 900 or 976 prefix), there is more opportunity to examine your current product lines and see if there are items associated with it that you can market in this fashion. Further, if you've compiled information of a proprietary nature that business might employ in a competitive environment, this information can be developed into concise reports and sold by telephone.

With the wide variety and use of telemarketing, the following steps should be followed in setting up a telemarketing program:

Objective. Is the objective a direct product sale, lead generation, conversion of inbound inquiries to sale, market research, inbound 800 number direct response, or reactivation of dormant accounts? Is the objective to cross-sell other lists or to work with another company's customer base?

Method. In *direct product sales,* the method is making outbound calls to a selected list of prospects or active leads to sell the product. In *lead generation,* you make outbound calls to qualify a list for interest before a follow-up by another salesperson. With *inbound inquiries,* the company trains customer service reps to acquire product knowledge for a cross-sale or add-on to the products a customer already has. In the *reactivation of dormant accounts,* outside telemarketing people, or inside salespeople, call a list of dormant accounts to stimulate prior customers' interest and regenerate sales activities. In *cross-selling,* the telemarketers call a group of customers who buy products that are related to the product being introduced in the sales effort. In *market research,* the company might structure a telephone survey to obtain interest level. With inbound *800 number response,* the company advertises products and has a direct response device for radio, print, or catalogs. People call in from ads they see in other direct response media.

Skill level. Skill level is different for each of these objectives and methods. Many times firms will need to bring in an outside consultant for a day or two, to help structure scripts and to instruct personnel on how to handle the telemarketing objective.

Reactivating accounts, calling preferred customers, and conducting market research can often be handled by current staff employees; however, there are companies that specialize in telemarketing and work out commission arrangements with clients on the sale of the product.

It is very critical to understand the skill level of the telemarketers. When selling a product directly, they need to be aggressive, able to make a high number of dials, and capable of closing a sale over the phone.

A company should not limit itself to working with salespeople and direct mail. Telemarketing should be considered to see if it can add an increased closing rate to your other direct response formats. (Direct mail by itself can generate a 2 to 5 percent response rate, but when coupled with a telemarketing follow-up, response can grow to 25 to 30 percent.) People rushing in and out need answers quickly, and they may not have time to come to a store to shop. A salesperson in touch with them can be a welcome selling proposition for any business. More and more consumers are shopping by phone, and if a business isn't alert to this, it may be losing its customers to just such telemarketing and direct mail tools.

Bibliography & Suggested Reading

LeBoeuf, Michael. *How to Win Customers and Keep Them for Life.* New York: Berkeley, 1989.

Levinson, Jay Conrad. *Guerilla Marketing: Secrets for Making Big Profits From Your Small Business.* Boston: Houghton Mifflin, 1993.

———. *Guerilla Marketing Excellence: The 50 Rules for Small-Business Success.* Boston: Houghton Mifflin, 1993.

Rapp, Stan, and Thomas L. Collins. *Maximarketing: The New Direction in Advertising, Promotion, and Marketing Strategy.* New York: Plume, 1989.

Ries, Al, and Jack Trout. *Bottom-Up Marketing.* New York: Penguin, 1990.

Sewell, Carl, and Paul Brown. *Customers for Life: How to Turn That One-Time Buyer Into a Lifetime Customer.* New York: Simon & Schuster, 1992.

Slutsky, Jeff, and Mark Slutsky. *Streetsmart Marketing.* New York: John Wiley & Sons, 1989.

Richard H. Johnson

Owner/Consultant—21st Century Marketing Systems Inc.

Since 1990, thousands of small businesses throughout the United States and Canada have experienced exponential growth in revenue and profit using the unique strategies found in the 21st Century Marketing Systems created by Richard Johnson.

In 1995, Richard developed a marketing consultant training package to teach other consultants and business owners how to implement the system themselves. Currently there are over 130 consultants using the system throughout the United States, Canada, and Germany.

Richard has a Masters in Business and, in addition to this book, has authored four other publications: *Your 21st Century Marketing Systems* Volumes One and Two, *Your Entrepreneurial Marketing Advantage*, *The New Entrepreneurial Professional*, and *The Entrepreneurial Employee*.

The marketing strategies taught in *Twenty Five Way to Increase Sales and Profits Without Spending an Extra Dime on Advertising* are contained within the 21st Century Marketing System.

Richard is committed to seeing that the marketing strategies found in his new book and the 21st Century Marketing System are used by small and medium sized businesses throughout the world.